Studio Craft & Technique for Architects

Second Edition

First published by School of Architecture UCD, 2011

LAURENCE KING

First published in Great Britain in 2015
Second edition published in 2022
by Laurence King Student & Professional
An imprint of Quercus Editions Ltd
Carmelite House
50 Victoria Embankment
London EC4Y 0D2

An Hachette UK company

FSC

MIX
Paper from
responsible sources
FSC® C008047

www.fsc.org

ISBN 978-191394-771-2

10 9 8 7 6 5 4 3 2 1

Design concept by Conor & David
Design of this revised edition by Detail.ie

Printed and bound in China by C&C Printing

A note on measurements

This book was originally created for
readers in Ireland and the UK. All
measurements are given in metric units.
Where appropriate, we have provided
straight conversions in parentheses for
readers in the US and elsewhere using
the I-P (Inch-Pound) system: metric (I-P).
Where US standard dimensions differ
from those in the British Isles, we have
indicated this by giving the standard
US dimension, rather than a straight
conversion. In some cases this is simply
indicated as: metric/I-P. In other cases
we have left units as metric only, where
it is not appropriate to provide a straight
conversion or where the principle being
discussed remains the same regardless
of unit of measurement.

I-P measurements are expressed using
the standard US convention. For example,
8 feet 6 inches is expressed as 8'-6".

Irish/UK convention for floor levels used
throughout: ground floor, first floor, etc.

Studio Craft & Technique for Architects

Second Edition

by
Miriam Delaney
& Anne Gorman

Advising Editor
Dr. Sarah A. Lappin

US Advisor for this edition
David Fannon

Contents

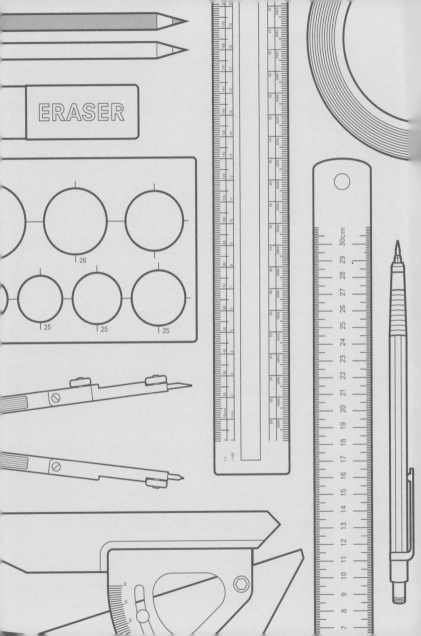

Foreword

Studio Craft & Technique for Architects was initially written in 2011 to assist students with the principles of architectural drawing conventions. Having decided to write a short 'pamphlet' to help our students, the book expanded as we felt it necessary to link the tools and techniques of drawing and model-making with the principles of design and construction. We believe fundamentally that architectural design and construction should be understood as intrinsically linked.

In this revised edition we address areas of increasing concern since the book was first written – most urgently, the impact that the climate crisis has had on our understanding of construction. Decisions about the selection and evaluation of building materials have changed significantly (Chapter 6), as have the ways in which we detail and construct buildings (Chapter 8). We have included a new section in Chapter 5 which looks at site analysis and strategies for the positioning and massing of buildings to maximize daylight, sunlight, ventilation and shelter. A heightened awareness of the environmental impact of construction pervades the revised text, as does our own experience of using this book as a teaching tool. We have added US terminology, standards and dimensions to make this publication more accessible to US students.

We would like to dedicate this book to Wendy Barrett, who taught us both, and whose exacting standards of architectural drafting and commitment to teaching architecture left an indelible mark on us and on generations of UCD architecture students. Thank you, Wendy.

Introduction
Tools of
the Trade

John Tuomey
Professor of Architectural Design
University College Dublin

Architectural education ought not to be compared to a craft training exercise, because unlike the craftsman who excels in making things already known, tried and tested, the architect must be educated to respond creatively when faced with unforeseen challenges. Yet we could never rely on an aspiring professional who lacked a practical mastery of the tools of the trade. Confidence comes with competence. Fluency comes with practice. In the studio we have to learn two things at once: to enquire and simultaneously to confirm, and to ask spontaneous questions and express our answers with demonstrations of skill. Learning by doing means that in trying something new, we test how much we already know.

The trained eye can measure a room. The trained hand draws without stopping to think. Drawing is thinking out loud. Paying attention to the material elements of the surrounding world, architects slowly acquire a reflexive understanding of space, construction, scale and dimension.

A lifelong acquisition process begins the first day we enter the first-year studio. We learn to sharpen a pencil, lean into the paper, draw a line on the page as if it is a profile in space. There is secret pleasure in all this patient work. The smell of the pencil, its weight in the hand, the freedom of finding out which way the drawing is taking us next. One line drawn suggests another.

This useful book is something to keep in your pocket. It is a beginner's guide that will lead you along clear and consecutive paths of applied learning. It is a book of basic principles. Practise these deceptively simple procedures until your analysis of buildings and places becomes inseparable from your appreciation, and the discipline becomes inherent in your own way of working.

1

Getting Started in Architecture

Craftsmanship arises from manual skill,
training and experience – personal
commitment as well as judgement.
—Juhani Pallasmaa

All the work of the hand is rooted in thinking.
—Martin Heidegger

As a starting point, this chapter will introduce you to the basic equipment you will use in your study of architectural design. We begin with an introduction to the tools you will use when drawing, and provide some tips on using your drafting equipment.

While there are many specialist drawing implements, the ones we cover here will allow you to complete accurate architectural drawings. We also introduce you to the tools and equipment used in a building laboratory. Again, there are specialist tools in the laboratory for cutting and model-making, such as the laser cutter and the C&C router, and the tools we deal with here will see you through your first two years of study. Finally, we look at common tools and techniques for making architectural models.

While this chapter gives you practical tips and advice, there is no substitute for experience. As you get used to drawing and model-making, you will hone your own methods and techniques, and, we hope, take pleasure in drawing and model-making – the foundations of architectural design.

1.1
Basic Equipment

1.1.1 Drawing Board & Parallel Motion

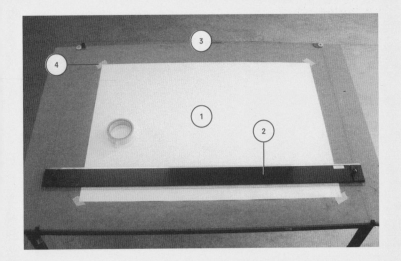

Fig. 1

1. Backing sheet
2. Parallel motion
3. Drawing board
4. Drafting tape

Screw the parallel motion to the drawing board – use the fixings at the top and bottom of the board to ensure the wire is held taut and secured in place.

Drawing boards come in various sizes and materials. The most common metric sizes are:

A0: working area of 1270 × 920 mm
A1: working area of 920 × 650 mm
A2: working area of 650 × 470 mm

Standard US dimensions are:
E 34 × 44"
D 22 × 34"
C 17 × 22"

Common materials include timber, MDF, plastic and melamine (which is a smooth plastic finish to a wooden base).

Parallel motions are preferable to T-squares because they allow greater accuracy and stability in drawing. 'Mayline' is a common brand name for parallel motions. Use the 'Mayline' to draw horizontal parallel lines.

Pre-assembled boards and parallel motions are available, which are easy to transport and come with an adjustable prop.

TIP

When fixing paper to the drawing board ensure the page is in line with (and parallel to) the parallel motion. The parallel motion should move smoothly in a 'parallel motion' along the board – it shouldn't wobble!

Use a brick or block of wood to prop up the board – it's easier to work when the board is at an incline.

Use graph paper covered with acetate as a backing sheet to guarantee a clean surface.

The graph paper allows you to easily align your paper. You can use the graph lines to set out text and lines when using transparent paper.

Secure each corner of the paper with drafting tape.

1.1.2 Adjustable Set-square

Set-squares are used for drawing vertical and inclined lines. The adjustable set-square is most useful as it can be set to any angle. The fixing screw allows you to set the angle of the set-square.

NB
Never use a scalpel with a set-square or Mayline – it will nick the edges and result in uneven lines when drawing.

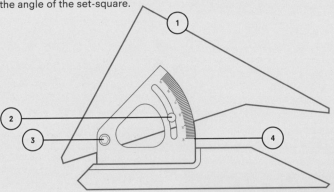

Fig. 2

1. Adjustable arm
2. Fixing screw
3. Hinge
4. Scale of degrees

TIP

Keep your set-squares and parallel motion clean using baby wipes or soap and water, and always wash your hands before starting to draw. Graphite dust from pencils can smudge drawings.

1.1.3 Clutch Pencil & Eraser

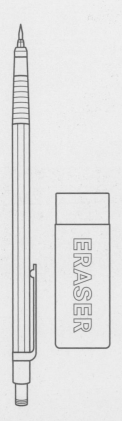

Pencil leads range from grades 9B to 9H. The most commonly used leads in architectural drawings range from grades 4B to 4H. The higher the 'B' number the softer the lead, and the higher the 'H' number the harder and sharper the line.

Architects typically use mechanical or 'clutch' pencils when drawing, because they allow greater precision than wooden pencils. Mechanical pencils are available in various thicknesses of lead. The most common are .5 or .7 mm. 'Clutch' pencils are mechanical pencils with thicker leads, which can be sharpened. The 2 mm clutch pencil is the one most commonly used for architectural drawing.

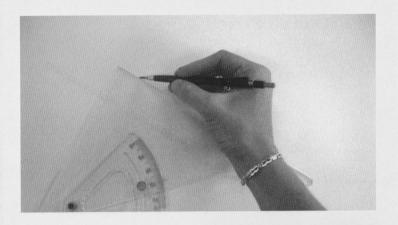

Work out the size of your drawing before you begin and position it on the page carefully. It helps to draft up a 'net' – a quick mock-up of the size and position of elements – on a separate page. Very light lines (construction lines) should be used to set up the position of the drawing on the paper.

TIP

Slowly turn the pencil as you draw along a set-square or Mayline; it leads to a more even line weight.

Start your drawing from the top and work down – the less you move the Mayline and set-square over the drawing the cleaner it will remain.

Keep your hands clean and touch the drawing as little as possible to avoid smudging.

Pencil lines should be clean, even and firm – avoid 'going over' lines and broken 'hairy' lines.

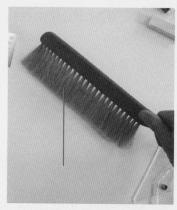

Fig. 3

1. Eraser shield
2. Drafting brush

On presentation drawings, use an eraser shield to erase small errors accurately while protecting the rest of your drawing.

Use a drafting brush after erasing to ensure the paper remains clean. This removes the residue from the eraser and stops it from smudging the drawing.

TIP

Putty rubbers are more effective on dark leads or charcoal drawings.

If using drawing ink, a sharp safety blade can remove ink marks from tracing paper. Mask one edge when using a razor – this takes a bit of practice!

Crumbs from the eraser can get lodged under the Mayline and cause marks on your drawing – clean the Mayline regularly.

1.1.4 Pencil Sharpeners

A wide range of pencil sharpeners are available for various kinds of pencils. For wooden pencils you can use the simple hand-held pencil sharpener (Fig. 4.1) or the mechanically operated rotary sharpener (Fig. 4.2), which gives a better point. Most narrow lead mechanical pencils (.5 mm – .7 mm) do not require a pencil sharpener, but for thicker lead clutch pencils a few options are available. As a basic option, some clutch pencil brands (such as Faber-Castell and Staedtler) come with a small built-in lead sharpener in the pushbutton of the pencil, or small plastic sharpeners are available to buy cheaply (Fig. 4.3). These are useful when you're out and about.

For a cleaner and more precise point use a rotary lead-sharpener (Figs 4.4, 4.5). These sharpen the pencil leads by rotating the pencil lead around an internal metal file.

Fig. 4

1. Simple wood-pencil sharpener
2. Rotary pencil sharpener
3, 4, 5. Pencil lead pointers

TIP

When using rotary lead pointers, dust on the pencil lead can smudge your drawings. Wipe the lead clean on a cloth before drawing. Alternatively, some pointers come with a small foam well you can dip the lead into.

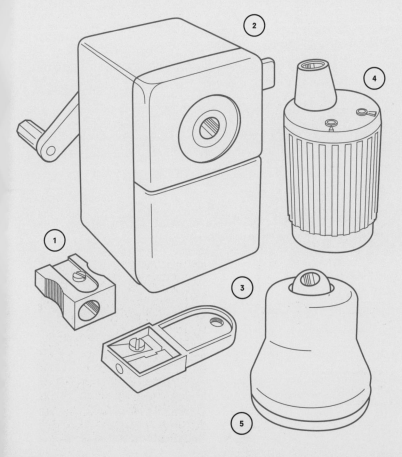

1.1.5 Compass

A compass is used for drawing circles and arcs of varying radii (Fig. 6). A pencil/pen attachment (Fig. 7) is used to draw circles with felt-tip pens or coloured pencils. A lengthening bar (Fig. 8) is used for drawing larger circles.

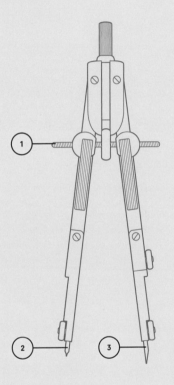

Fig. 5

1. Adjustment screw
2. Needle point
3. Pencil lead

TIP

Keep both the needle point and the pencil lead perpendicular to the paper surface. Both arms of the compass are hinged for this purpose.

Additional leads are available for compasses to allow you to match the line weights on your drawing.

Fig. 6

Fig. 7
1. Pencil/pen attachment

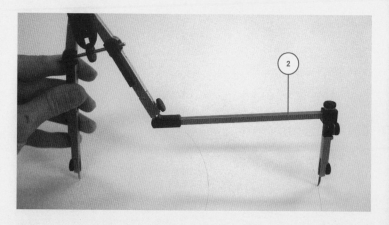

Fig. 8
2. Lengthening bar

1.1.6 French Curves

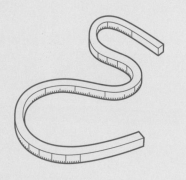

French curves are plastic templates used for setting out complex curves. Use the French curve by rotating it until you find an arc/curve that aligns with the points you want to join.

An alternative to French curves is the 'flexi-curve' – a length of pliable plastic. This requires some patience and practice, but can be useful for drawing repetitive curves.

1.1.7 **Circle Templates**

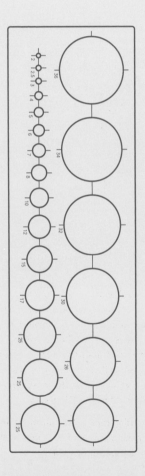

For drawing small circles, use a circle template as the compass becomes too fiddly on small diameters.

NB
Do not draw curves – including door swings – freehand on a technical drawing. Always use a compass or circle template.

1.1.8 Drafting/Masking Tape

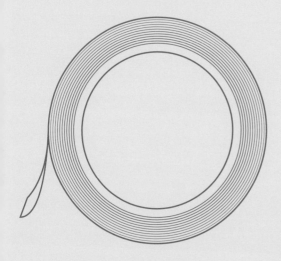

Masking tape is a type of pressure-sensitive tape made of a thin and easy-to-tear paper, and an easily released adhesive, allowing it to be removed without leaving residue or damaging the surface to which it is applied. It is available in a variety of widths, ranging from 10 mm to 50 mm (⅜" to 2").

Drafting tape is less strong than masking tape and so is less likely to tear paper or card.

1.1.9 Colouring Pencils

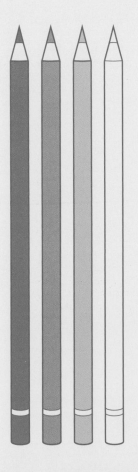

There are three common categories of colouring pencil; oil-based, wax-based and water soluble. Wax-based are widely available, but oil-based are better quality for architectural drawings. Faber-Castell's 'Polychromos' colouring pencils are recommended for high-quality pigment and soft leads which allow for easy blending of colours. Other cheaper brands will not give the same results.

1.1.10 **Sketch Book**

Fig. 9

Fig. 10

Sketch books (Fig. 9) are used to document projects. Images and articles can be pasted in as support material. A wide variety of sketch books are available. Hard-cover sketch books are the most practical as they are hard-wearing and provide a solid base on which to sketch. A5 (smaller) sketch books are recommended because they are easily portable.

Moleskine brand notebooks are useful as they have a pocket (Fig. 10) to store leaflets, images, etc. They come in a range of sizes and paper types, including graph paper, plain sketch books and lined notebooks.

See **Section 4.1.3** for examples of how architects use sketch books.

TIP

Use a sketch book with heavy cartridge paper – it allows you to use different media, such as pencil, ink or light watercolour.

Do not use a lined sketch book.

1.1.11 Scale Rule

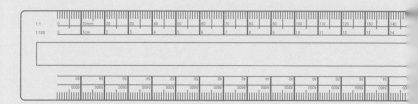

A scale defines the relationship between the original object and the drawing or model. The original scale, 1:1, is the full size of the object.

Most scale rules contain the following common architectural and engineering scales:

1:1 and 1:100
1:20 and 1:200
1:5 and 1:50
1:1,250 and 1:2,500

Common scales for drawings in I-P units are:

3″	=	1′-0″
1½″	=	1′-0″
1″	=	1′-0″
½″	=	1′-0″
¼″	=	1′-0″
⅛″	=	1′-0″
¹⁄₁₆″	=	1′-0″

You can use your scale rule for measuring off drawings at bigger scales by moving the decimal point. For example, use the 1:50 scale to measure drawings at 1:500, but add a zero to get the correct dimension.

Scale rules are available as flat two-sided or triangular three-sided rulers. We advise that you start with a flat scale rule as they are easier to get used to. As you grow more experienced, try the triangular scale rule, which has the advantage of more scales shown. Triangular rulers are available in I-P and metric units.

See **Section 2.1** for more
information on common
drawing scales.

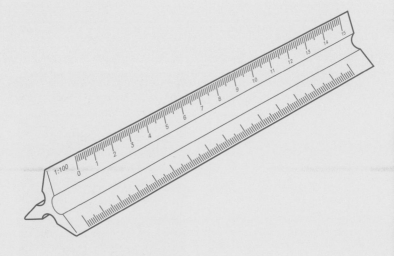

1.1.12 **Scalpel & X-Acto Knife**

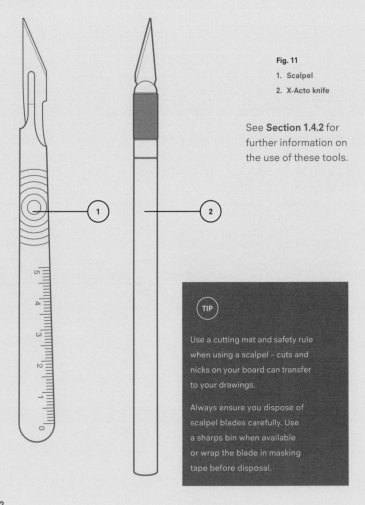

Fig. 11
1. Scalpel
2. X-Acto knife

See **Section 1.4.2** for further information on the use of these tools.

TIP

Use a cutting mat and safety rule when using a scalpel – cuts and nicks on your board can transfer to your drawings.

Always ensure you dispose of scalpel blades carefully. Use a sharps bin when available or wrap the blade in masking tape before disposal.

1.1.13 Sketch Paper & Steel Rules

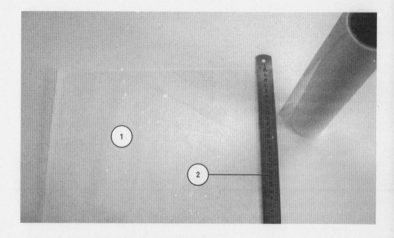

Sketch paper is semi-transparent and used for sketching and tracing. It comes in sheets (sometimes called 'butter paper') or in rolls of varying sizes. Using a roll when overlaying hard-line drawings allows you to sketch freehand but keep your drawings to scale, enabling you to try out many options quickly.

A steel rule is a metal ruler used as a cutting edge in model-making, as it does not get damaged by the scalpel or knife. Cork-backed steel rules resist slipping.

Fig. 12
1. Sketch roll
2. Steel rule

1.1.14 Drawing Pens

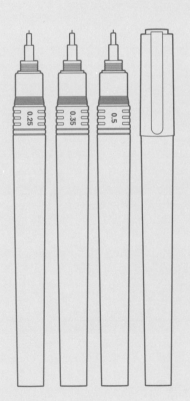

Drawing pens or **drafting pens** are rarely used these days, but would have been commonplace in drawing offices until the mid-1990s. They require a lot of care and maintenance, but when a level of skill is developed a very high level of drawing quality is possible. Rotring is a commonly available brand of drafting pen.

1.1.15 Fine Pens

Fine pens come in varying nib thicknesses, from 0.1 mm to 2 mm. 0.2 mm and 0.5 mm are the more commonly used sizes.

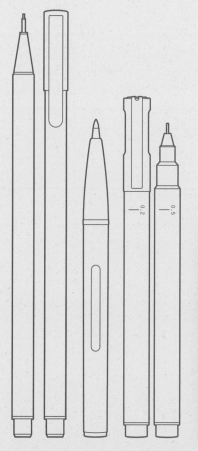

> **TIP**
>
> Fine pens are most suited to sketch detailing, where a detail can be worked up using overlays of sketch roll to test different versions of a particular detail.
>
> Never use fine pens for hard-line drafting as they are not capable of the line quality required for such drawing.

1.2
Paper Types & Line Weights

1.2.1 Paper Types

At first glance, there appears to be an infinite amount of paper to choose from when it comes to drawing — or drafting as it is sometimes called.

As architects and students of architecture, we need to become familiar with paper types and the media that most suit them. This will come with experimentation and experience. In the meantime, we have put together some basic information to help you on your way.

The following pages list the basic paper types you will use in your first year of college.

Paper is graded according to its weight in grams relative to 1m² of paper.

Typical office photocopy paper is 80g/m². Paper weights used for drawing purposes range from 25g/m² to 300g/m².

The unofficial unit symbol **gsm** (meaning **g/m²**) is also widely used in English-speaking countries and can be found on most reams of photocopy paper.

In the US paper weights are measured in what are known as basis weights by the pound.

Paper is also graded according to a measurement known as 'tooth'. This refers to the degree of surface texture of a given piece of paper and is normally determined by how the paper is made and the material used to make it.

Standard ISO Paper Sizes
The advantage of the ISO system is its ability to scale without compromising the aspect ratio from one size to another. If a sheet with an aspect ratio of $1:\sqrt{2}$ is divided into two equal halves parallel to its shortest sides, then the halves will again have an aspect ratio of $1:\sqrt{2}$.

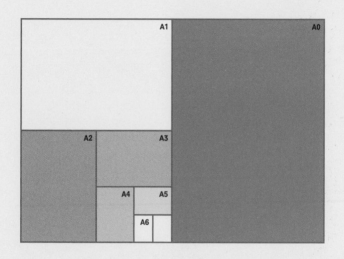

A-Series	millimetre
A0	1188 × 840 mm
A1	840 × 594 mm
A2	594 × 420 mm
A3	420 × 297 mm
A4	297 × 210 mm
A5	210 × 148.5 mm
A6	148.5 × 100 mm

US sizes

Name	inches
Letter (ANSI A)	8.5 × 11 "
Tabloid (ANSI B)	11 × 17 "
Arch C	18 × 24 "
Arch D	24 × 36 "
Arch E	36 × 48 "

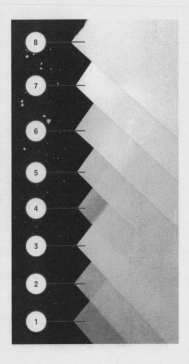

Sketch Paper

Like a lot of paper types, sketch paper comes in both sheet and roll form. A4 sketch paper roll is most typically used and is a staple of studio work.

At 25 g/m² this is the lightest paper you will use and it is generally suited to freehand sketching and overlaying. Tear off an A3-sized section and place it over your hard-line or sketch drawings. The transparent nature of the paper allows tracing and re-working of earlier drawings.

Fig. 13

1. Sketch paper
2. Butter paper
3. Detail paper
4. Tracing paper
5. Vellum
6. Cartridge paper
7. Watercolour paper
8. Watercolour paper

(TIP)

Always write your name on the paper edge side of your rolls, because they can go missing in a studio environment.

Butter Paper

This comes in sheets slightly smaller than A1 at 750 × 500 mm. It is more durable than sketch roll, with a weight of 40 g/m². It has an off-white yellowish colour.

It is useful for overlays, sketching and setting-out drawings or 'nets'. It is not typically used for presentation drawings because it is non-standard size.

Detail Paper

This is typically used as part of the design process and is less common for finished drawings. It is a delicate paper and pretty unforgiving in that it is difficult to correct/erase lines once they have been drawn.

It is generally used in sheet form at A1 size (840 × 594 mm). It could be described as semi-opaque (partially see-through).

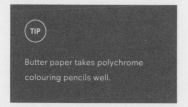

TIP

Butter paper takes polychrome colouring pencils well.

Tracing Paper

This comes in three common weights: $63\,g/m^2$, $90\,g/m^2$ and $112\,g/m^2$. It is available in pad, sheet and roll form. It was traditionally used for working drawings and presentation drawings because it takes pencil and drawing pens well. It was widely used as it could be copied on a dyeline machine, which is an old form of the modern-day printer. It is an excellent litmus test for developing your drawing skills, and for this reason we would recommend it.

Vellum

This is a semi-opaque high-quality paper used for the purpose of presentation. It has a slightly oily feel and is more forgiving than detail paper (see p. 41) when it comes to minor adjustments.

Vellum paper is becoming very difficult to get nowadays because it is no longer widely produced.

TIP

Keep your hands clean when using tracing paper, as greasy paper will repel ink or cause smudging and poor line quality.

Never use fine pens or markers on tracing paper as they are not capable of the same line definition that is possible with pencil or drawing/drafting pens (e.g. Rotring Rapidograph/Staedtler Mars).

Cartridge Paper

Like tracing paper, cartridge paper comes in all the standard sheet sizes. Typically it is available in weights of 110 g/m², 155 g/m² and 200 g/m². It is used for presentation drawings and the thicker, better-quality papers take ranges of pencil lead weights particularly well.

Cartridge paper is opaque and off-white in colour. You cannot trace onto cartridge paper unless you use a light box.

Watercolour Paper

This differs from manufacturer to manufacturer, so experiment not only with the different kinds of paper but also with various brands.

Weights range from 190 g/m² to 600 g/m². There are three different types of finishes available, which relate to the process by which they are made: rough, cold-pressed and hot-pressed paper. Hot-pressed has a smooth finish that takes colour and lead pencil and pastel very well. It is particularly suited to rendering finished drawings with these media.

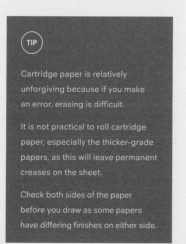

TIP

Cartridge paper is relatively unforgiving because if you make an error, erasing is difficult.

It is not practical to roll cartridge paper, especially the thicker-grade papers, as this will leave permanent creases on the sheet.

Check both sides of the paper before you draw as some papers have differing finishes on either side.

1.2.2 Line Weights

Architectural drafting requires different skills and techniques compared with freehand artistic drawings. Drawing techniques are learned over time by practice and with the application of the discipline of shared standards and conventions.

All basic drawing skills are born out of a competency in pencil drawing. As mentioned in Chapter 1, the clutch pencil is the staple of pencil drawing. It holds a 2mm-diameter lead, which is slotted into the tip-end of the pencil's metal casing, as demonstrated here.

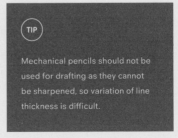

TIP

Mechanical pencils should not be used for drafting as they cannot be sharpened, so variation of line thickness is difficult.

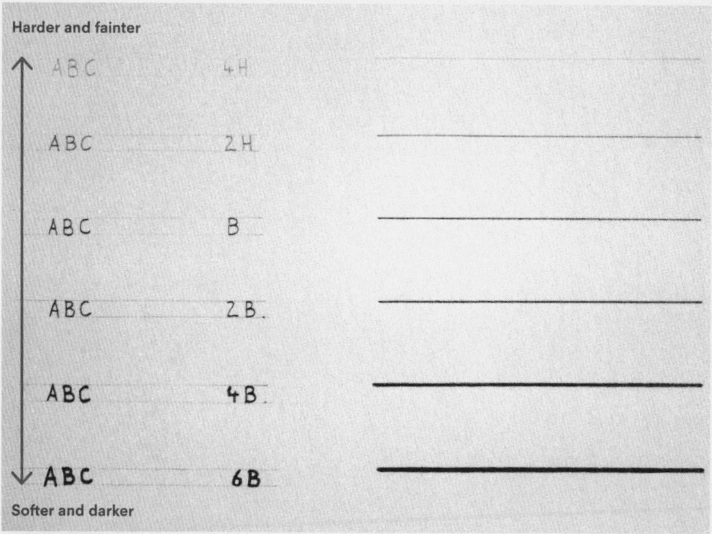

Harder and fainter

A B C	4 H	
A B C	2 H	
A B C	B	
A B C	2 B	
A B C	4 B	
A B C	6 B	

Softer and darker

Lead types most commonly used for drafting are HB, B, 2B and 2H. Sometimes a 4H is used for fine hatching and construction lines. The higher the 'H' number the harder the lead will be; conversely, the higher the 'B' number the softer the lead will be. This is illustrated above with a selection of the most commonly used leads.

It is helpful to have at least two clutch pencils available at any time so you can have two different leads ready for use. The HB and the 2B are the most useful leads for setting-up construction lines and for hard-line drawings, because you can get a good range of line thicknesses with a minimum amount of lead sharpening.

1.3
Building Laboratory

Most schools of architecture have a model-making workshop or building laboratory, which provides students with the facilities and tools to make scale models, to test building materials or to make large-scale constructions. Facilities vary widely from school to school, so here we outline common tools and equipment that are widely available.

Safety is paramount in the building laboratory, and students must follow instructions on using the equipment. In your first year of study, you will be introduced to safety procedures to follow in the lab.

No student should attempt maintenance of the machines. If you experience difficulty, always contact the building laboratory manager. When using machinery in the workshop, always wear appropriate PPE (see section 1.3.1); wear closed-toe shoes; tie back your hair; and don't wear loose clothing, scarves or ties which could get caught in machinery.

1.3.1 Personal Protective Equipment (PPE)

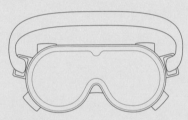

Dust mask

NB
Always wear a **dust mask** when
using machinery that generates
dust or fine particulates – such as
the belt sander – or when cutting
fibrous material such as softboard.

Safety goggles

NB
Always use **safety goggles** when
cutting metal on the bandsaw,
drilling metal or cutting masonry
with a chisel.

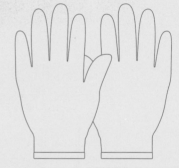

Ear protectors

NB
Always use **ear protectors** when using any loud machinery in the building laboratory.

Gloves

NB
Always use **gloves** when mixing concrete or working with raw timber, which may have splinters. Gloves should also be used when cutting metal, as jagged edges and burrs can be dangerous.

1.3.2 Saws

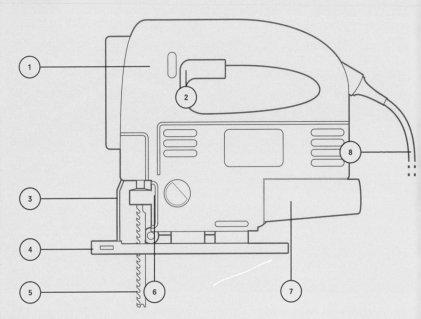

Fig. 14

1. Trigger lock
2. Control trigger
3. Blade holder
4. Base plate *or* shoe
5. Blade
6. Orbital action adjuster
7. Vacuum connection
8. Power lead

The jigsaw is used for cutting timber, metal or acrylic.

Change blades and speeds depending on the material you are cutting. Lower speeds are suitable for harder materials such as metal and acrylic.

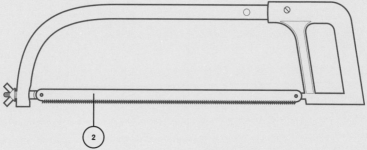

Fig. 15

1. Timber saw
2. Hacksaw

NB

The hacksaw is the only hand saw suitable for cutting metal. Never use a coping saw or fretsaw for cutting metal, or you will break the blade.

Always check which tools you are allowed to use in the studio.

1.3.3 Hammers & Mallets

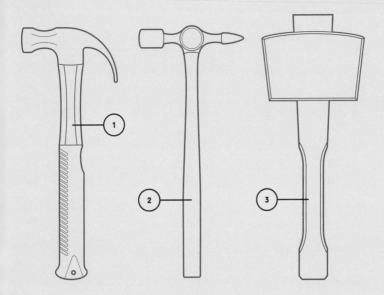

Fig. 16

1. Claw hammer
2. Cross-peen hammer
3. Wooden mallet

Hammers and mallets are tools designed to deliver an impact to an object. Their most common uses are for driving nails, fitting parts and breaking up objects. The wooden mallet is used for driving chisels.

1.3.4 Combination Square

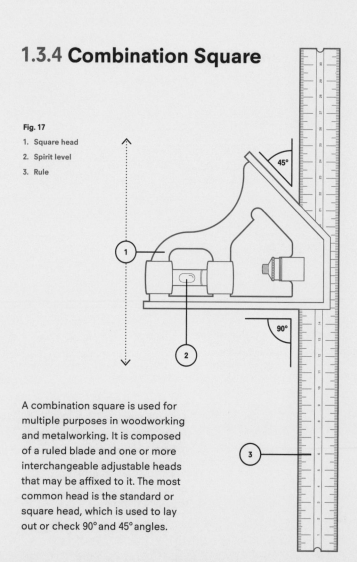

Fig. 17

1. Square head
2. Spirit level
3. Rule

A combination square is used for multiple purposes in woodworking and metalworking. It is composed of a ruled blade and one or more interchangeable adjustable heads that may be affixed to it. The most common head is the standard or square head, which is used to lay out or check 90° and 45° angles.

1.3.5 Tri-square & Sliding Bevel Gauge

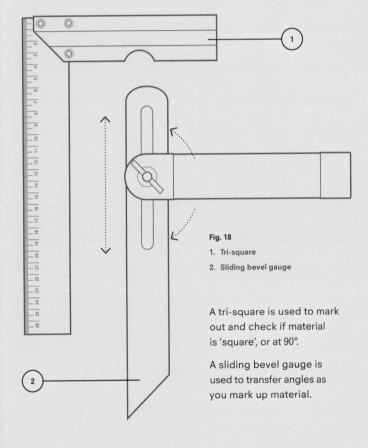

Fig. 18

1. Tri-square
2. Sliding bevel gauge

A tri-square is used to mark out and check if material is 'square', or at 90°.

A sliding bevel gauge is used to transfer angles as you mark up material.

1.3.6 Screwdrivers

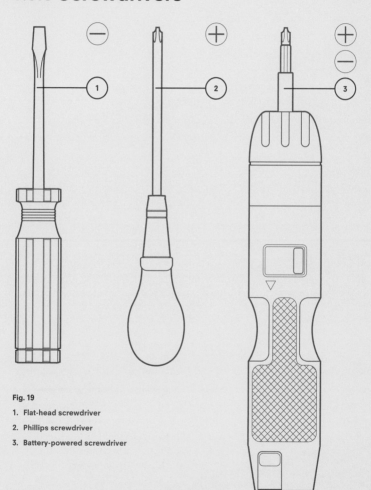

Fig. 19

1. Flat-head screwdriver
2. Phillips screwdriver
3. Battery-powered screwdriver

1.3.7 Pliers

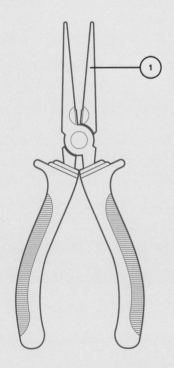

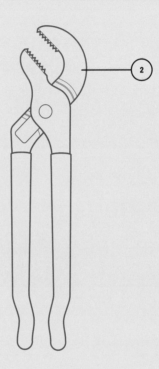

Fig. 20

1. Needle-nose pliers
2. Water-pump pliers

Pliers are used to hold objects firmly, usually for cutting, bending or physical compression. The jaws can be used to manipulate objects that are too small to be held with the fingers.

1.3.8 Chisels

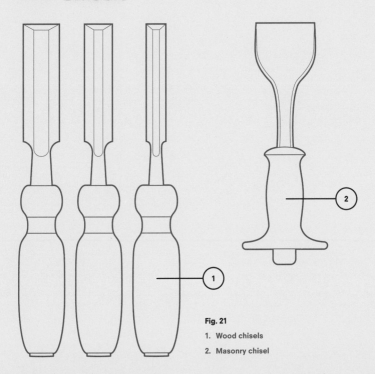

Fig. 21

1. Wood chisels
2. Masonry chisel

Chisels are used in conjunction with mallets to chip or gouge out wood or masonry (and, less commonly, metal).

NB
Always use eye protection when working with chisels.

Only use the chisel recommended for the material you are working on. Never use a wood chisel on masonry or metal.

1.3.9 Spirit Level

Fig. 22
1. Vertical (plumb) indicator
2. Horizontal (level) indicator
3. 45° inclination indicator

A spirit level is an instrument designed to indicate whether a surface is horizontal (level) or vertical (plumb) or at an angle of 45°.

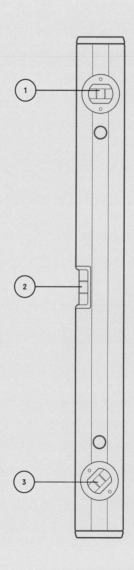

1.3.10 Utility Knife

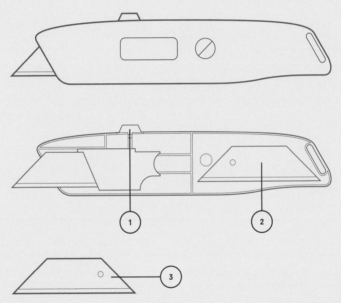

Fig. 23

1. Blade retractor
2. Storage compartment
3. Blade

The utility knife is used for cutting and scoring material such as heavy-duty card, lightweight metal, thin sheets of Perspex and foam.

It is less accurate than a scalpel for model-making, but stronger and more suitable for building lab work.

NB
Always use a cutting mat and safety ruler with a scalpel or knife.

1.3.11 **Bandsaw**

Bandsaws can be used for cutting timber, metal or Perspex. Low-speed bandsaws are suitable for metal and Perspex; high-speed bandsaws are for timber.

NB
Using a high-speed bandsaw for metal is dangerous. If you are unsure of the appropriate speed, check with the lab manager before starting.

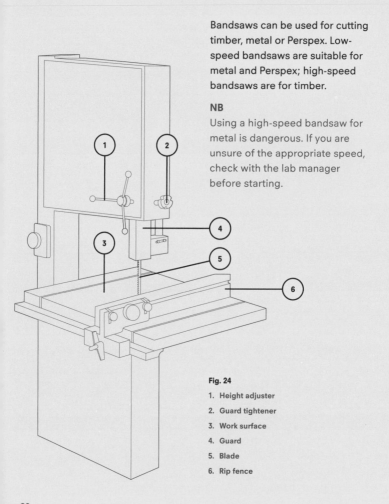

Fig. 24

1. Height adjuster
2. Guard tightener
3. Work surface
4. Guard
5. Blade
6. Rip fence

Fig. 25

1. Mitre guide
2. Fence

Use the mitre guide and fence to hold the material in position as you cut it. The mitre guide can be fixed to allow you to cut at an angle.

NB
Always lower the guard as close as possible to the material you are cutting.

It is best practice to always wear safety goggles when using any cutting or drilling machines in the building laboratory.

1.3.12 Guillotine

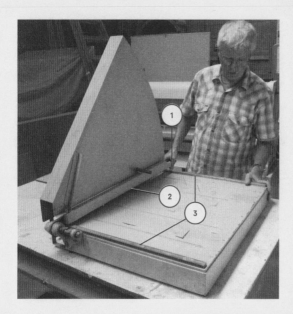

Fig. 26

1. Lever
2. Blade
3. Guides

Use the guillotine for cutting paper or card. It is very useful for cutting a number of sheets together.

Align the paper or card with the guides. The lever is attached to a heavy blade. Lower the lever to cut the card.

NB
All guillotines are designed for right-handed use, so take extra care if you are left-handed as they take a bit of getting used to.

1.3.13 Belt Sander

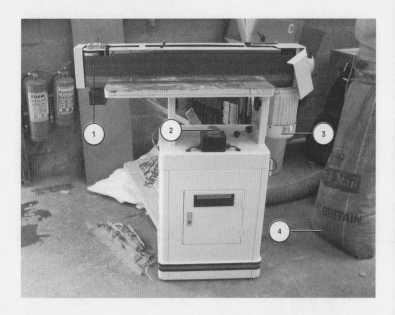

Fig. 27

1. Sandpaper belt
2. Controls
3. Motor
4. Extractor bag

NB

Use the belt sander for timber only. Never use metal on the sander as sparks from the friction of the sandpaper and metal may travel to the extractor bag and cause the dust to catch fire.

Never wear loose-fitting clothes or scarves when using the belt sander. They could become tangled in the machine and prove fatal.

1.3.14 **3D Printers**

3D printers allow for a whole new world of possibilities, creating intricate scaled models and prototypes for new and inventive forms, junctions and so on – the list is endless. ABS/PLA 3D printers use thermoplastic filaments to create three-dimensional objects.

A 3D digital CAD model is replicated by heating the filament and printing the exact form in layers. Accuracies of 0.1 mm and greater are possible.

Fig. 28

Metal object made using a laser melting printer, metal powder, heat and 3D CAD data

Fig. 29
ABS 3D printer

1.3.15 Laser Cutters

Laser cutting provides a superior quality and finish not possible with card cut by hand, with clean cut edges, producing extremely fine contours and precision cutting in card of varying thicknesses. It can also be used on a variety of materials including metals, wood and acrylic sheets of certain thicknesses.

Fig. 30

Laser cutting machine

Fig. 31

Laser-cut card model

1.3.16 Foam Cutter

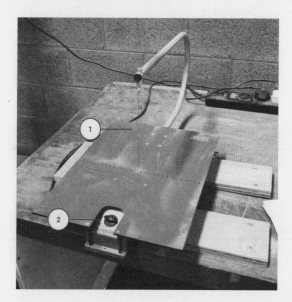

Fig. 32

1. Cutting wire
2. Controls

The foam cutter works by pressing the foam against a hot wire. The heat dissolves the foam and allows you to cut through it. Guides can be used to direct the foam as you push it against the wire.

See **Section 4.4.9** for tips on making foam models.

> **TIP**
>
> Move the foam slowly to avoid putting too much pressure on the wire. It could snap!
>
> Only use the foam cutter in well-ventilated areas.

67

1.4
Model-making Equipment

The most common model-making equipment is covered here, but be aware of other possibilities. Look at shops and suppliers other than those specifically aimed at model-makers. You can find great materials everywhere. Various metals are available in sheet and dowel form at specialist model shops and hardware shops. Other materials useful in making models include felt, cloth, resin, cork, foam, wire and acrylic.

Experiment! There are a huge range of possibilities in model-making. Take into account the type of model you are making. Quick sketch models can be very useful at the outset of a project, whereas large-scale presentation models are usually made at the end of complex projects.

The type of material you use can determine how you develop your design. For example, cast models are very useful to help you get a feel for cast materials such as concrete.

1.4.1 Glues

Acrylic Resin Glue
This is a fast-acting acrylic resin that has great bonding strength, sometimes referred to as 'super glue'.

Care is needed.
Not suitable for card or paper.

Clear Synthetic Resin
This glue dries clear and is temporarily adjustable before setting.

Glues paper, cardboard and Styrofoam.

Wood Glue

Various brands are available. This all-purpose glue works well with card, balsa, foam and paper. It dries clear.

Not suitable for metals or plastics.

Spray Mount

This is used to mount drawings – e.g. fixing paper onto a card background. If used in moderation you can separate the paper from the card later to reposition or remove if required.

Suitable for card and paper only.

71

PVA Glue

This is a good everyday glue.
It is not as strong as wood glue.

Suitable for card and paper only.

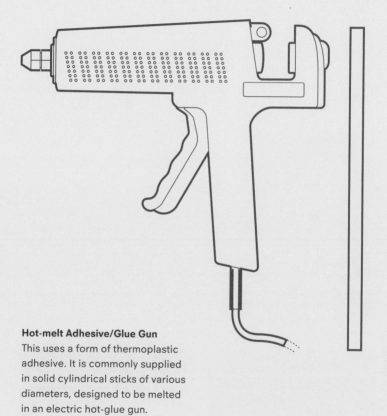

Hot-melt Adhesive/Glue Gun
This uses a form of thermoplastic
adhesive. It is commonly supplied
in solid cylindrical sticks of various
diameters, designed to be melted
in an electric hot-glue gun.

Not suitable for metals.

1.4.2 Scalpels

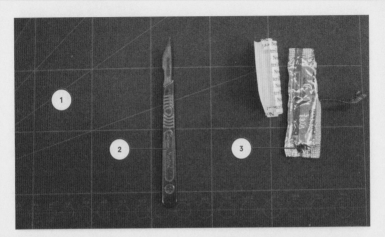

Fig. 33

1. Cutting mat
2. Scalpel
3. 10A blades

Scalpels are suitable for cutting paper, card and balsa wood. For harder materials, a Stanley knife or utility knife can be used, but it is harder to maintain accuracy. The blade should not move. A wobbly blade is dangerous and inaccurate.

NB
Scalpel knives are a very dangerous piece of equipment. Never put your fingers in the blade path, and be sure to learn how to use a scalpel from an experienced user. Change your blade often for safety and to maintain accuracy.

TIP

Your cutting mat can warp if stored in a vertical position. Always store it horizontally.

1.4.3 Other Equipment

Modelling Clay

This is very useful for quick sketch models, but difficult to achieve precision with. It is available in a range of colours.

Plaster of Paris

This is very useful for making cast models – see step-by-step details in **Section 4.4.14**.

1.4.4 Balsa & Bass Wood

Balsa and bass wood are common model-making materials. Both are light and easy to cut. Bass wood is denser but less rigid than balsa, and is more readily available in the US, while balsa is more commonly used in Ireland and the UK. Both woods are ideal for light, stiff structural elements in model-making. Make sure you work *with the grain* in balsa, as this will give the model strength.

The density of dry balsa wood ranges from 40–340 kg/m³ (2–21 lbs/ft³) with a typical density of about 160 kg/m³ (10 lbs/ft³).

Balsa comes in sheets, square sections and circular sections.

Balsa Sheets: 910 × 76 mm

Standard thicknesses:
0.8 mm
1.5 mm
2.5 mm
3 mm
5 mm

In the US, balsa sheets come in a variety of widths, and a wide range of thicknesses starting at ¹⁄₁₆" Common lengths are:
24"
36"
48"

TIP

Balsa can be stained to achieve darker colours. It is best to do this when the model is complete to ensure that edges are coloured.

Square Balsa Sections:
910mm (long) × various square
and rectangular profiles

Standard profiles:
1.6 × 1.6mm
2.4 × 2.4mm
3.2 × 3.2mm
3.2 × 4.8mm
3.2 × 6.4mm
4.8 × 4.8mm
4.8 × 6.4mm
6.4 × 6.4mm

Square Balsa Sections:
910mm (long) × various square
and rectangular profiles

Standard profiles:
1.6 × 1.6mm
2.4 × 2.4mm
3.2 × 3.2mm
3.2 × 4.8mm
3.2 × 6.4mm
4.8 × 4.8mm
4.8 × 6.4mm
6.4 × 6.4mm

1.4.5 Board/Card

Grey Card

This is a cheap and basic model-making material. It has a matt finish and is grey throughout – therefore you will not have a problem with a core showing through at the joints of a model. It is useful for contour models and takes spray paint well, so it can be painted once the model is complete.

Foamboard/Foamcore

This is composed of two very thin sheets of card with a foam centre. It is available in 3mm and 5mm thicknesses, in white or black. It is easy to cut but is not flexible, and is therefore useful for making models of orthogonal shapes.

Ivory Board

This is a very thin, white flexible card. It has a matt finish on one side and a slightly glossy finish on the reverse. It is useful for quick sketch models and fine details, such as window tracery. The matt side tends to yellow over time.

Corriboard

This is a translucent and non-flexible plastic sheet material with a hollow core and inner corrugations. It is difficult to work with, but can be useful for representing opaque materials, such as Reglit (profiled glass).

Brown Card

This is a thin sheet material that is cheap and easy to cut, and is therefore useful for quick models. It is also useful for lining large-scale models to indicate changes in building material.

Mounting Board

This comes in a variety of colours, with a white backing. It is quite difficult to cut and the edges tend to yellow over time, so it is not ideal for models.

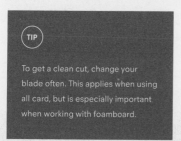

TIP

To get a clean cut, change your blade often. This applies when using all card, but is especially important when working with foamboard.

2

Principles of Representation

Recognition of the drawing's power as a medium turns out, unexpectedly, to be recognition of drawing's distinctness from and unlikeness to the thing that is represented, rather than its likeness to it, which is neither as paradoxical or as dissociative as it may seem.
—Robin Evans

In this chapter we introduce you to the principles of architectural representation. The most common types of architectural drawings are two-dimensional depictions of three-dimensional space; these are called orthographic projections.

Architects also use a number of 3D scaled drawing techniques to explain their buildings; the most common types are discussed here – isometric, axonometric and oblique projections. These are very useful tools that allow you to explain your proposals in three dimensions.

Perspective drawings give the illusion of real depth and are useful techniques for getting a sense of what your design would be like as a built reality.

Drawing with a range of representation types can help you develop your design, because each type of representation allows you to explore different aspects of your proposal.

The types of drawings you choose to present your work are critical to explaining your proposals properly. Always plan in advance which type of drawings will most accurately portray your intended design.

2.1
Scale

An **enlarged scale** shows the object 'blown up' (e.g. at 5:1 the drawing will show the object five times larger than the actual size). In architectural drawings this can be useful for small elements, such as ironmongery (hinges, door handles, window latches, etc.).

A **reduced scale** shows the object smaller than the original size. For example, a scale of 1:50 will show the object or building 50 times smaller than the real size. Most architectural drawings are shown at a reduced scale.

Metric is the most common global measuring system, with length measured in millimetre (mm), centimetre (cm) and metre units (m). Inch-Pound (I-P) is commonly used in the USA, with the units of

length being inch, foot, yard and mile. An inch is 25.4mm, but for ease of conversion we usually assume 25mm. Similarly, 1m is 3'-4".

Many metric dimensions evolved from I-P measurements, which historically were more widely used. For example the standard size of many sheet materials – 2,440 × 1,220mm – relates to the I-P dimension of 8 × 4'.

Use your scale rule for measuring off drawings and for setting up your own scale drawing. Scale rulers are available in either metric or I-P units.

Common Scales for Architectural Drawings

1:500 or 1:1,000	Site plans or overall block layout plans
1:250	Overall plans or site plans
1:200	Overall plans
1:100	General arrangement drawings and layout plans
1:50	Working drawings
1:25	More commonly used by engineers
1:20	Construction plans – room layouts and details
1:10	Detail drawings – e.g. door and window schedules
1:5 or 1:2	Technical details

Common scales in the US are:

1/16" = 1'-0"	(similar to 1:200)
1/8" = 1'-0"	(similar to 1:100)
1/4" = 1'-0"	(similar to 1:50)
1/2" = 1'-0"	(similar to 1:20)
1" = 1'-0"	(similar to 1:10)
1½" = 1'-0"	
3" = 1'-0"	

NB
Never make up your own scale,
such as 1:40, just to fit your
drawings on a page.

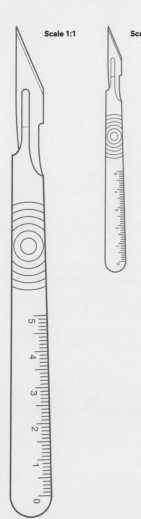

Scale 1:1 **Scale 1:2** **Scale 1:10**

Scaling on a Photocopier

With the rise of computer-aided drawing programmes, it has become much easier to alter the scale of scanned images digitally. It is useful, however, to know the formulae to scale drawings on a photocopier. These formulae can be used for scaling your own hand drawings or for adjusting drawings you have printed.

The formula to enlarge or reduce the scale of a drawing is:

(original scale/required scale) × 100

For example: Assuming your original drawing is 1:50, and you want to enlarge it to 1:20:

(50/20) × 100 = 250%

You would magnify your 1:50 drawing by 250% to convert it to 1:20.

Or if you want to reduce your 1:20 drawing to 1:50:

(20/50) × 100 = 40%

If, however, you do not know the scale of the original drawing (which is often the case with published images), it is still possible to bring the drawing to a working scale.

Example

Say you require a scaled plan at 1:100. If you know the dimension of a particular element or room in a building (which may be mentioned in the text), e.g. that a specific room is 6,000 mm long, but on your copy of the drawing it measures 5,300 mm (using the 1:100 side of your scale rule), you can bring the drawing to scale with this formula:

(required dimension/current dimension) × 100

So:

(6,000/5,300) × 100 = 113%

If you do not know a 'true' dimension on the drawing, you can still attempt to bring the drawing to a working scale.

For example: A standard internal door in a domestic setting is often 900 mm wide. Assuming that to be the case, you can use the above formula to bring the drawing to scale. It is best to check this with a number of elements.

NB

This method should be used with a lot of caution, because you are making an assumption about standard sizes that may not be true and could result in inaccurately scaled drawings.

Scaling a drawing up/down on the photocopier

2.2
Orthographic Projection

Orthographic projection is a means of representing three-dimensional objects in a two-dimensional drawing. Most drawings of buildings consist of two-dimensional views called plans, sections and elevations. Understanding the principles and techniques of orthographic projection is a fundamental skill for an architect, and allows you to communicate your ideas to other architects, clients and builders.

The conventions of orthographic projection are universal; plans, sections and elevations are legible across languages and cultures.

Orthographic projections can be difficult to understand at first as they do not replicate how the human eye sees the world- there is no foreshortening. However, orthographic projections remain to scale, and so are extremely useful. In **Section 2.4** we deal with perspective, which is a representation type that tries to reproduce how the eye sees.

2.2.1 Common Orthographic Projections

Plan View

A plan is a horizontal cut through the building, showing a downward view of the room layout. A plan typically shows internal wall configurations, furniture and external elements such as windows and doors.

The horizontal cut through the building that determines what we see in the plan is usually taken at 1–1.5m above the floor level (3–4' in the US). This usually allows windows and doors to appear on the plan.

The height at which you choose to set your plan is known as the cutting plane. While 1–1.5m is typical, you can choose to have a higher or lower cutting plane in order to view certain elements within your design. Because 1–1.5m is the standard, if you deviate from this you should state it clearly on your drawings.

Plan views are identified according to the floor they apply to – e.g. Ground Floor, First Floor, etc.

A *roof plan* represents the view of the building as it is seen from above, and is often used on a site or location plan.

A *reflected plan* shows the upward view of the interior of the building – e.g. looking towards the ceiling rather than the floor. This type of plan is useful when indicating lighting layouts, structural elements or roof lights.

Section

This type of projection is created by making a vertical cut through a building. Sections are very useful for understanding internal circulation, heights of rooms and the vertical relationships between spaces.

Sections can be selected to show a detail (e.g. of a wall construction), or show the whole building, or cut through the building on its site. The latter is called a site section.

The position of the vertical cut that you make to construct the section should be clearly labelled on all plans.

Sections are particularly useful in understanding the organisation of buildings. We recommend *Manual of Section*, by Lewis, Tsurumaki and Lewis.

See **Section 3.1.2** for information on drawing annotations.

Elevation

An elevation is a vertical view, typically of the exterior appearance of a building. The projection lines are drawn at right angles from the plan, onto the page surface. Elements that are curved or angled are not seen at their true lengths in elevations.

Elevations are usually labelled according to their orientation on the plan: north, south, east or west. An elevation may show the external or internal view of a building or room.

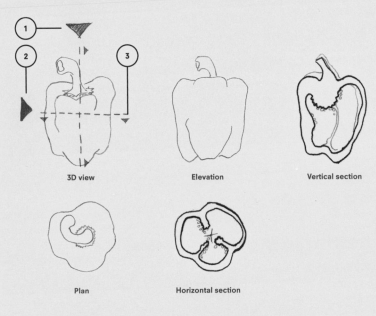

3D view

Elevation

Vertical section

Plan

Horizontal section

Fig. 34

1. Arrow indicates the
   downward view – the plan.
2. Arrow indicates the straight-on
   front or side view – the elevation.
3. Dashed lines indicate the
   imaginary cuts where the section
   is taken – vertical and horizontal.

Case Study: **O'Flaherty House**

O'Flaherty House, Kinsale, County Cork

Architect: Robin Walker, 1967

In order to explain the principles of orthographic, three-dimensional and perspective drawings, we will use the O'Flaherty House by Robin Walker as our template.

This house is a beautifully designed Modernist pavilion, with a simple square floor plan.

93

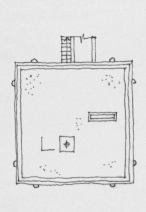

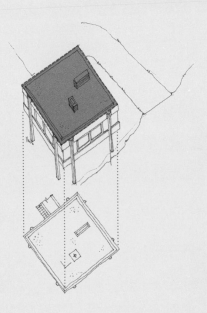

Roof Plan

The roof plan is the view of the building looking directly down on the roof. Roof plans are commonly incorporated into site or landscape drawings.

Three-dimensional View

See **Section 2.3** for constructing three-dimensional projections.

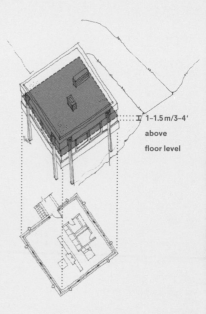

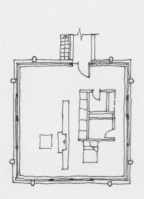

I⋯⋯ 1–1.5 m/3–4'
above
floor level

Floor Plan

The floor plan is a horizontal cut through the building, looking down. You set the height at which you want to take this section; the common height is 1–1.5 m above the floor level (3–4' in the US). Any elements such as walls, furniture or openings that are cut will appear darker as 'section lines'.

Elements that are not cut (i.e. below the line at which you take the cut) will appear lighter.

Elements that occur above the cut line are indicated as a broken line. See **Section 3.1.1** for information on line types.

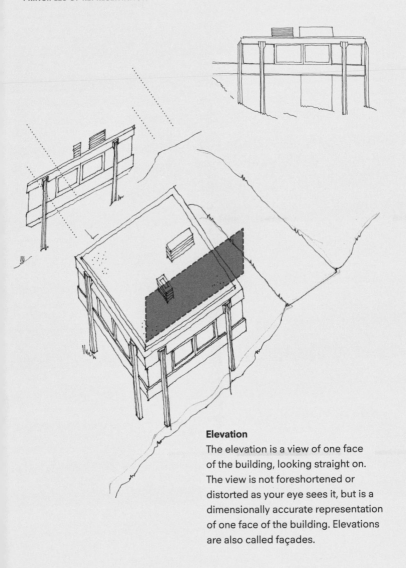

Elevation

The elevation is a view of one face of the building, looking straight on. The view is not foreshortened or distorted as your eye sees it, but is a dimensionally accurate representation of one face of the building. Elevations are also called façades.

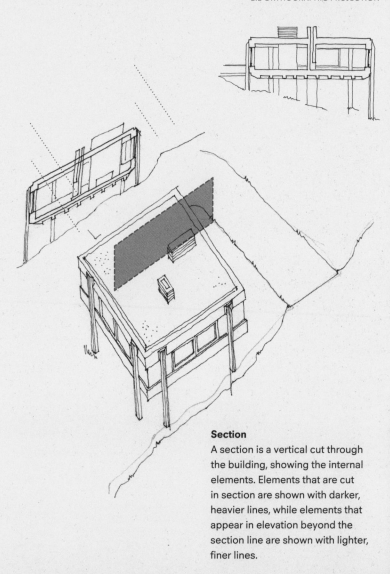

Section

A section is a vertical cut through the building, showing the internal elements. Elements that are cut in section are shown with darker, heavier lines, while elements that appear in elevation beyond the section line are shown with lighter, finer lines.

2.3
Three-dimensional Projections

Axonometric, isometric and oblique projections are commonly used architectural conventions, which are collectively known as 'paraline' drawings. They are relatively simple to produce and are good techniques to represent the mass, internal spaces and proportions of buildings. They do not, however, produce 'realistic' perspective views. Parallel lines remain parallel in paraline drawings, whereas in perspective drawings, parallel lines converge. We deal with the conventions of perspective drawings in **Section 2.4**.

A significant advantage of paraline drawings is that the scale remains true, so you can measure to scale off the drawings.

Line weights should be carefully used in paraline drawings. Major elements should be emphasized with heavier line weights, and minor elements, such as furniture or finishes, should be drawn in lighter lines.

Variations on paraline drawings (such as 'exploded', 'worm's-eye' or 'cut-away' drawings) can be very useful to explain your projects. See examples in **Chapter 4: Working Through Drawing**.

2.3.1 Types of Projection

Drawing plane

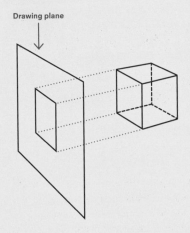

Orthographic
Orthographic projections are two-dimensional drawings of three-dimensional objects where the drawing plane is parallel to the main plane being depicted and the projection lines are perpendicular to it.

See **Section 2.2** for further explanation.

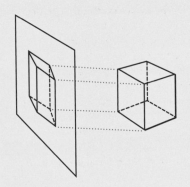

Oblique
Oblique projections are two-dimensional drawings of three-dimensional objects where the drawing plane is not always parallel to the main plane being depicted and the projection lines are never perpendicular to it. Types of oblique projections include plan oblique and elevation oblique.

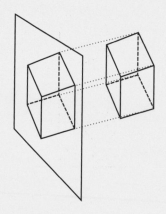

Axonometric

Axonometric projections are two-dimensional drawings of three-dimensional objects where the drawing plane is not parallel to the main axes of the object being depicted and the projection lines are perpendicular to it. Scale remains true but curves and circles are distorted. Isometric projection is a type of axo where the axes are equally foreshortened.

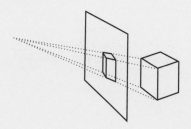

Perspective

In a perspective projection lines converge at a single point outside the drawing plane. The object being depicted is foreshortened and not to scale.

For a more detailed explanation of perspective, see **Section 2.4**.

2.3.2 Drawing Circles and Curves

Circles and curves are straight-forward to construct in most paraline projections. The exception is isometric projection, where the two axes of the circle are not at right angles. So, an ellipse must be constructed.

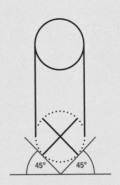

Axonometric Projection
Circles remain true and are not distorted. Axonometric angles vary.

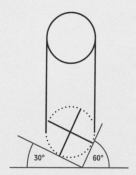

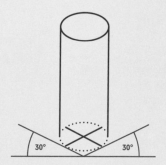

Architect's Projection
Circles remain true and are not distorted.

Isometric Projection
Circles are distorted and must be constructed as ellipses.

2.3.3 Drawing a Building in Axonometric Projection

Step 1
Draw your plan and elevation to scale. If you are constructing a cut-away or internal axonometric, a section is also necessary in order to calculate internal dimensions.

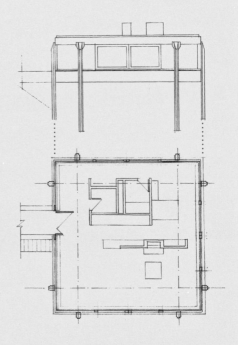

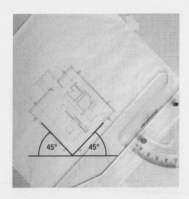

Step 2
Rotate the plan drawing on your drawing board. In this example we are rotating to 45°.

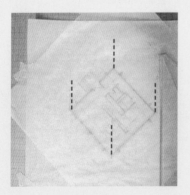

Step 3
Overlay a piece of sketch paper over your plans and draw vertical lines up from all corners in your plan.

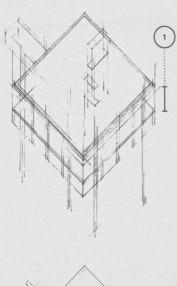

Step 4

All vertical dimensions remain true, so measure the heights off your elevation and mark them on the vertical lines you have drawn.

Using light construction lines, connect the vertical lines at the correct height with lines drawn at 45°.

Fig. 35

1. True height – as measured to scale off the elevation

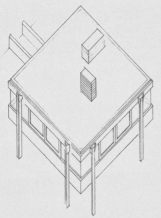

Step 5

Trace neatly over your 'net' construction drawing to produce the finished drawing.

Exploded Axonometric

You can extrude the elements of your axonometric to reveal the internal world of your building or to highlight structure or circulation. This is called an exploded axonometric, and is a very informative drawing.

Fig. 36

1. You determine the distances between the 'exploded' elements; there is no rule for this. You should, however, pull the elements far enough apart to make them clearly visible.

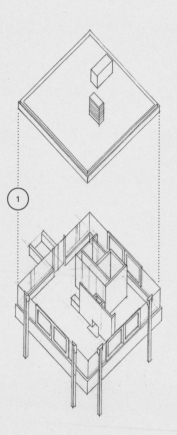

2.4
Perspective

Perspective drawings aim to reproduce how the human eye sees three-dimensional spaces. Perspectival techniques were developed by artists such as Filippo Brunelleschi during the Italian Renaissance. These techniques had a radical impact on Renaissance art, and the original mathematical principles are still used when constructing perspective drawings today.

The significant difference between paraline three-dimensional drawings and perspective drawings is that the latter show parallel lines converging and elements foreshortened. Think of how train tracks converge in the distance when you view them straight on. Because of the foreshortening and distortion associated with perspective drawings, you cannot take scale measurements from perspective views.

Perspective drawings are a very useful tool to help you to 'get inside' your designs and understand how they will appear and feel in the real world. Most people untrained to 'read' architectural drawings find perspectives easier to understand than orthographic or paraline drawings. For this reason, they are particularly useful for explaining your projects to clients and to the public.

2.4.1 Types of Perspective

One-point Perspective
In one-point perspective there is
one fixed point where lines recede
to, called the 'vanishing point' (VP).

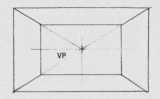

This type of perspective is useful for
simple interior views. Instructions
are given in **Section 2.4.2** on how to
construct a one-point perspective.

Two-point Perspective
There are two fixed VPs in two-point
perspective.

This type of perspective is useful for
both interior and exterior drawings.

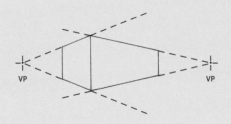

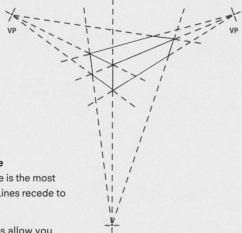

Three-point Perspective

Three-point perspective is the most complex to construct. Lines recede to three fixed VPs.

Computer programmes allow you to make quick three-dimensional models. These are particularly useful for massing and block models. It is still useful, however, to understand the principles underlying graphic perspective before you take on computer modelling.

Slight variations exist in the construction methods for perspective drawings. See the 'References & Further Reading' section at the end of the book for alternative construction techniques.

2.4.2 Drawing a Room in One-point Perspective

Step 1

Fix the viewing position in the room. This is called the 'station point' (SP). This is where the imaginary viewer stands in order to 'see' your perspective.

The 'cone of vision' (CV) sets the viewable area from the station point selected. It is generally assumed to be a 60° cone. Areas beyond this cone will be distorted in the perspective drawing.

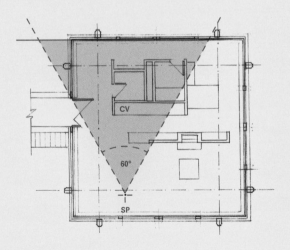

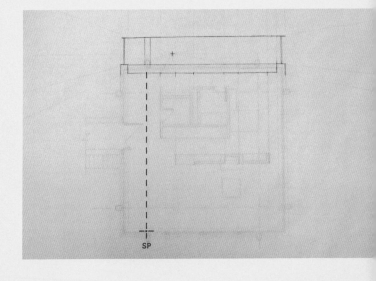

SP

Step 2

Draw an end elevation to scale of the room you are going to illustrate with one-point perspective. This is an internal elevation of the wall facing the viewer at the station point. This will form the backdrop of the perspective and is the only element in the final perspective drawing that remains to scale.

Step 3

Project a vertical line up from the SP onto the end elevation you have drawn.

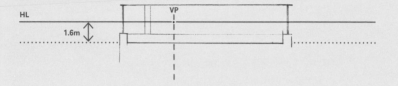

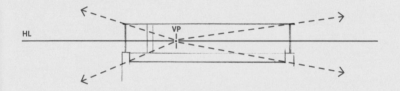

Step 4

Draw a horizontal line at eye level (typically 1.6 m/5' above the ground level). This line is called the 'horizon line' (HL). You determine the height of the HL. For example, if you want to construct your perspective from a child's viewpoint, you may set the HL at 1 m/3'.

The intersection of the HL and the vertical line projected from the SP on the plan is the VP of the end elevation.

Step 5

From the VP draw lines through the corners of the section to set up the room in perspective.

Reminder:
VP = vanishing point
HL = horizon line
SP = station point

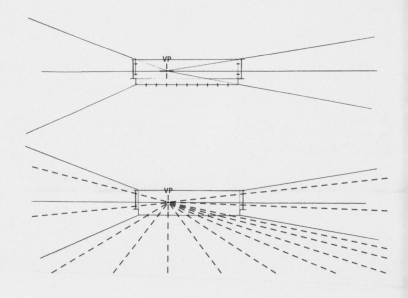

Step 6
On the end elevation mark out 1 m intervals along the ground line and vertical line, at the same scale as the elevation was constructed.

Step 7
Draw a series of light construction lines from the VP through the 1 m intervals.

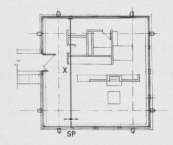

Step 8

On the plan, measure the distance from the SP to the end elevation — this is shown as X on the plan.

Transfer this distance at the same scale onto the HL, to the left of the VP.

Mark this point on the HL.

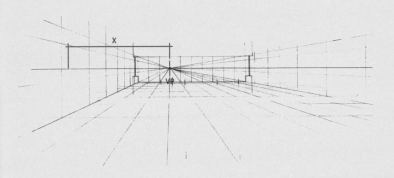

Reminder:

VP = vanishing point

HL = horizon line

SP = station point

Step 9

Draw a diagonal line from the point on the HL through the bottom left corner of your end elevation.

Fig. 37

1. Diagonal line through the bottom left-hand corner

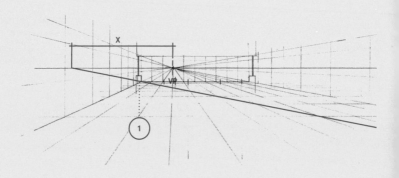

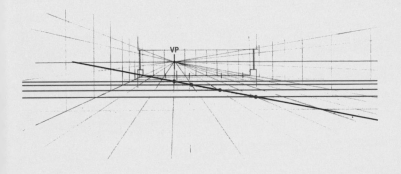

VP

Step 10

Where the diagonal line intersects with the lines projecting from the VP, draw a series of horizontal parallel lines.

This gives you a framework of 'tiles' which sets up your perspective. Each of these tiles represents an area of 1 × 1 m on the plan.

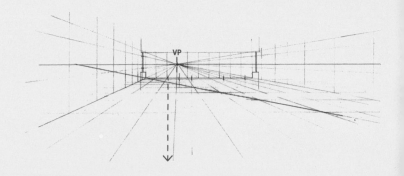

Step 11

Now mark off on the baseline
of your end elevation the position
of internal elements and furniture –
projected up from the plan.

Also mark the height of these
elements to scale on the vertical
edge of the end elevation.

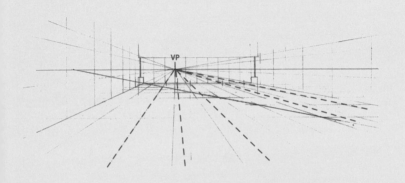

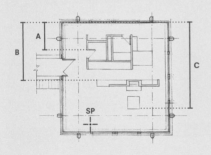

Step 12
Now draw lines from the VP through the points you have marked on the baseline.

Step 13
Measure the distances from elements on the plan to the end elevation/picture plane (e.g. A, B, C).

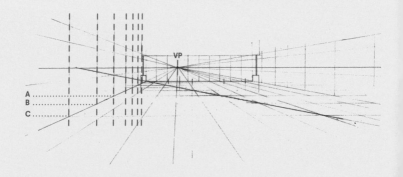

Step 14
Remembering that each division along the left-hand side equates to 1 m on your plan, mark off the position of the furniture or internal elements.

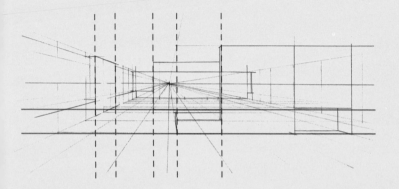

Step 15

Using the grids you have constructed, draw in any internal elements or furniture you want to include – always checking the height off the vertical scale bar on your end elevation.

Step 16
Trace over your net – either freehand or hard-line. This eliminates all unnecessary construction lines.

Step 17
You can then render the perspective with colouring pencils, watercolour or other media. Or you can collage in the background, figures and materials.

2.4.3 Selecting the Vanishing Point

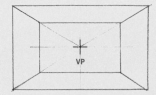

Drawing A

As noted in the previous example, take care when selecting the height and position of your vanishing point because it will have a significant influence on the area shown in the final perspective.

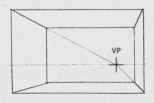

Drawing B

Drawings where the vanishing point is central (Drawing A) can result in symmetrical and quite dull drawings. A lower viewpoint can be effective if you want to emphasize the ceiling (Drawing B), while a high viewpoint emphasizes the floor (Drawing C).

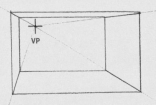

Drawing C

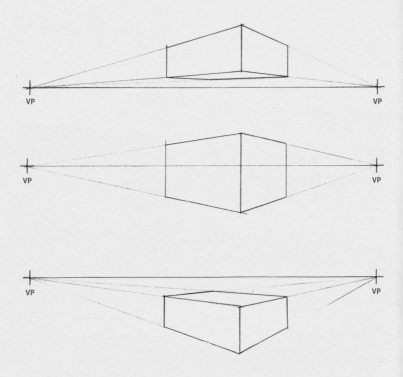

Similarly, consider the position of the object relative to the vanishing points in two-point perspective. You can choose to emphasize the roof, floor or walls, depending on how the vanishing points relate to the horizon line. The most realistic perspectives are those where human eye level is taken as the horizon line.

2.4.4 Freehand Sketch Perspectives

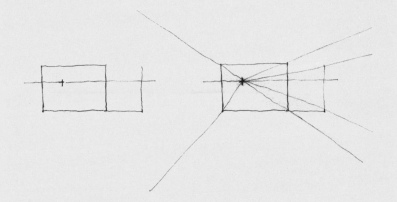

Use the same principles in order to construct very quick sketch perspectives as part of your design process.

Sketch the room's end elevation and mark a vanishing point.

Connect this point to the corners of the room in order to make the 'frame' of the perspective sketch.

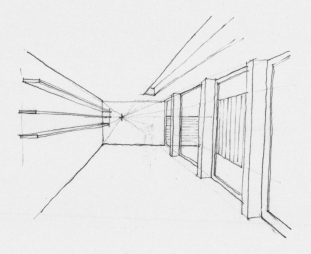

Now fill in furniture, columns, etc.
This method is not very accurate,
but use your eye to get approximate
spacings of elements – allowing for
foreshortening and compression.

These kinds of sketches are very
quick, and with some practice
proficiency is easily attained.

One-point street views (*opposite*) can be useful for drawing existing conditions or placing your proposal in context.

Use the same method to construct freehand two- or three-point perspectives (*above*).

3

Drawing Techniques

There is no distinction between a
drawing of construction and a thought
of construction. This correlation turns
drawings into the most sophisticated
expressions of architectural theory.
—Marco Frascari

As you get used to the tools and principles of architectural representation, it is important to know the conventions of architectural drawing. Architectural conventions – for representing materials, understanding scale, knowing how and when to add dimensions and notes to your drawings, and how to indicate elements such as windows, doors and stairs – allow your drawings to be understood by others. They also allow you to 'read' the drawings of other architects.

The conventions of architectural drawing have developed over centuries and constitute a language in their own right. A clear understanding and application of these conventions allows your design intentions to be legible and clearly understood – whether by a tutor in college or a builder on site.

Like any language, it takes practice to achieve fluency. As a student of architecture, you should get into the habit of using these conventions from the outset. They will soon become second nature to you and will give clarity to your own designs.

3.1
Drawing
Annotations

3.1.1 Line Types

Standard Line

This should be a clear, even line of medium darkness – a 2H lead works well for this. It is typically used for drawing elevations.

Section Line

This is shown as a strong, dark line – an HB lead works well for this.

Construction/Setting-out Line

This line should be as light as possible – use a hard H lead, such as 4H.

Dash-dot Line

This indicates a cutting plane.

Broken Line

This is used to show what is overhead or underneath.

Centre Line

This is used to indicate an axis, or centre line.

Break Line

This is used to show that the drawing includes only part of an element.

300 mm   750 mm

Dimension Line

This should be relatively light. Use 45° 'ticks' to mark off the lengths.

TEXT

Leader Line

This line refers text and notes to the relevant part of a drawing.

Contour Lines

Contour lines are used on maps and large-scale plans to indicate changes in level.

Check what the contour spacing represents – depending on the scale of the drawing, the spacing between contours can represent varying changes in level. For example: at 1:500 contours might represent spacings of 2m, while at 1:50 contours might represent spacings of 0.5m.

Void Line

Overhead voids are indicated with a faint 'x' mark. Dashed lines show overhead elements, such as light wells or roof lights.

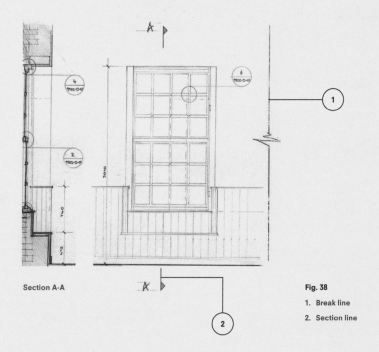

Section A-A

Fig. 38

1. Break line
2. Section line

Here, break lines are used
to indicate that the building
continues and is not shown in full.

The point at which a section is
taken is indicated with two small
arrows and the reference name
– sections are commonly named
with letters of the alphabet.

3.1.2 Drawing Annotations

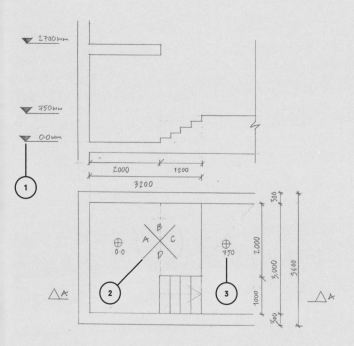

Fig. 39

1. Floor level indicator on elevations/sections

2. Naming system for internal elevations

3. Floor level indicator on plans

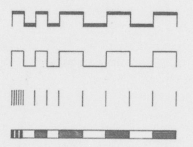

Scales

These are only used where the drawing is to be reproduced at a different scale to the original or where a number of scales are used within one drawing.

NB

Keep the scale as simple and legible as possible.

Section Arrows

Always indicate on your plans where the sections are cut with section arrows. The arrows should always point in the direction the section is facing.

Where you are drawing a number of sections, indicate the section lines with letters, e.g. Section A-A.

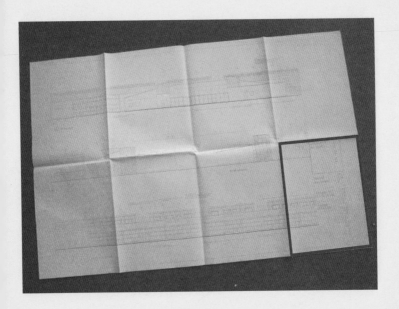

Fig. 40

A1 sheet – title block in

lower right-hand corner

Plan in advance where the title block will fit within the finished sheet. In working drawings, it is common to fold them to an A4 size to fit in files or folders. The title block should sit in the lower right-hand corner so it will be visible on the folded drawing.

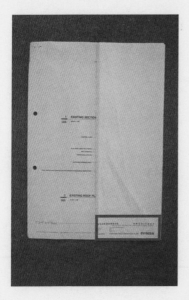

Fig. 41
A3 sheet – title block in
lower right-hand corner

Similarly, an A3 drawing will often
be folded to A4 size – so make
sure the title block is visible when
folded. (See p. 39 for table of
standard US paper sizes.)

3.1.3 Dimensioning (Plans)

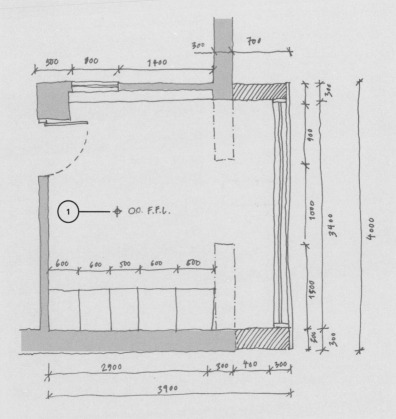

Fig. 42

1. Symbol for floor level

F.F.L. (finished floor level) on ground-floor
plans is normally taken as the 0.00 height.

Dimensions are normally written in millimetres (mm), except for large-scale site plans, where metres (m) are more suitable.

Some people in the building industry use Inch-Pound (I-P) units, but European architects always use the metric system (metres, millimetres, etc.). In I-P units, dimensions are normally written as a combination of feet and inches, using marks for the units and often a dash between them (for example 3'-6").

Write the measurement of the dimension parallel to the element being measured. As far as possible, place the dimensions outside the drawing for clarity. Indicate overall dimensions at the outside edge, with smaller chain dimensions running closer to the drawing.

3.1.4 Dimensioning (Sections)

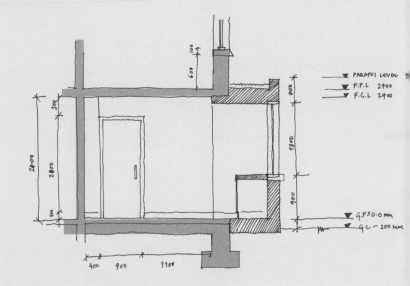

Fig. 43

G.L. (external ground level)

G.F. (ground floor)

F.F.L. (finished floor level)

F.C.L. (finished ceiling level)

When noting key heights or vertical dimensions, overall dimensions should be indicated with a short line and triangle with the dimension written alongside.

Again, place dimensions outside the drawing for clarity, and align levels and text.

3.1.5 North Points/Arrows

Every plan should indicate the orientation of the building. This is shown by an arrow pointing in the direction of north.

Drawing conventions suggest that plans are drawn orthogonally, with the north oriented towards the top of the page. If possible keep to this convention, as it makes drawings easy to read.

TIP

Keep the north symbol simple to avoid it dominating the drawing.

3.1.6 Sheet Planning

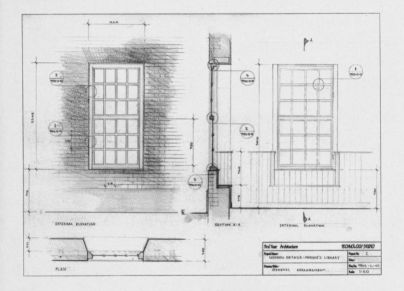

The elevation is typically drawn directly above or below the plan.

Plans should read in sequence: left-to-right, top-to-bottom or bottom-to-top. Do not mix up the sequence of your plans, as this can cause confusion.

TIP

It is useful to align elevations and sections, both for ease of construction of the drawing and for ease of understanding.

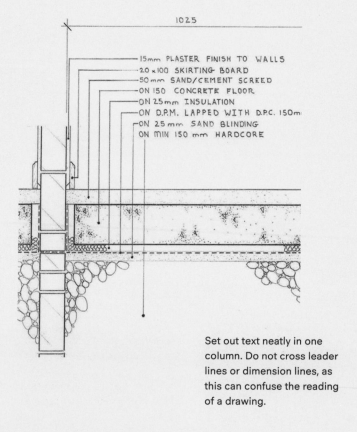

1025

15mm PLASTER FINISH TO WALLS
20 x100 SKIRTING BOARD
50 mm SAND/CEMENT SCREED
ON 150 CONCRETE FLOOR
ON 25mm INSULATION
ON D.P.M. LAPPED WITH D.P.C. 150m
ON 25 mm SAND BLINDING
ON MIN 150 mm HARDCORE

Set out text neatly in one column. Do not cross leader lines or dimension lines, as this can confuse the reading of a drawing.

3.1.7 Title Blocks

PROJECT NAME	DRAWING TITLE
NAME: AUTHOR	SCALE: 1:20
DATE: 01/09/09	DWG NO: 001·A
REV:	

Fig. 44

PROJECT NAME		
DRAWING TITLE		
NAME:	AN. ARCHITECT	
SCALE:	1:100	
DATE:	01·09·09	
DWG NO:	01·001·A	
REV	DESCRIPTION	DATE
A	FLOOR PLAN GF.	01·08·09
B		

Fig. 45

Every **working drawing** (construction drawing) should have a **title block** (Figs. 44–45) in the bottom right-hand corner, containing:

1. Project name
2. Drawing title
3. Author name
4. Scale
5. Date
6. Drawing number

You can format the title block to suit the page orientation – landscape or portrait.

PROJECT NAME			DRAWING TITLE	
REV.	DESCRIPTION	BY: DATE	DRAWN BY : AUTHOR	
A	- CHANGE TO ENTRANCE	M.D. 01 09	SCALE :	1:1
B	- ROOF LEVEL CHANGE	MD 04 09	DATE :	01 / 09 / 09
C	-		DRAWING NO. : 001·A·	
			CHECKED BY :	

Fig. 46

In architectural offices title blocks will also contain a **revision block** (Fig. 46). When a drawing such as a plan is edited and updated, it is given a revision reference – e.g. A, B, C, etc.

Each revision entry should describe briefly the main element of the revision and the date that the drawing was re-issued under the new revision reference. Also included is a 'checked by' section on the title block. The project architect will normally review the drawing before it is issued.

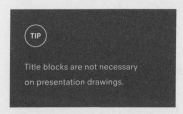

TIP

Title blocks are not necessary on presentation drawings.

3.2
Stairs
& Ramps

The dimensions and detailing of stairs and ramps
are typically controlled by national building codes
or regulations. The dimensions and standards in
this chapter comply with UK and Irish standards,
but should be checked in other jurisdictions.
In the USA always refer to the Americans with
Disabilities Act Standards for Accessible Design
(www.ada.gov). The examples in this section
mainly represent residential construction. Codes
and requirements for public buildings may differ.

3.2.1 Terminology

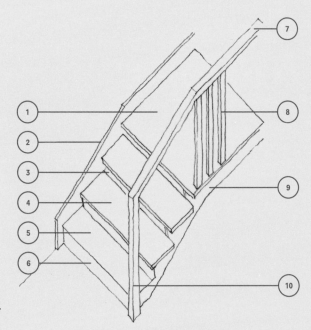

Fig. 47

1. Landing
2. Wall stringer
3. Open riser
4. Tread
5. Going (see p. 154 for detail)
6. Solid riser
7. Handrail
8. Balustrade
9. Outer string
10. Newel post

3.2.2 **Balustrades & Guard Rails**

Fig. 48

1.   < 100mm (4") maximum opening
     between balustrades

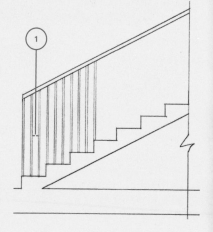

The dimension between the vertical or horizontal members of a balustrade must be less than 100 mm (4"). This is to prevent a child's head getting caught in the balustrade.

The 'less than 100 mm' rule also applies to the maximum gap between open-riser treads on stairs in a residential context.

Where the total rise of the stairs is less than 600 mm (24"), no handrails or balustrades are necessary in a private residence.

If the stairs are less than 1 m (3') wide, a handrail at one side only is sufficient. Where the stairs are 1 m (3') wide or wider, handrails are required on both sides. ADA standards require handrails on both sides in public buildings in the US.

3.2.3 Building Regulations

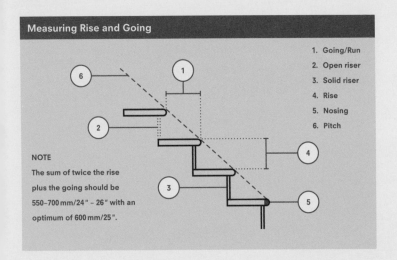

Measuring Rise and Going

1. Going/Run
2. Open riser
3. Solid riser
4. Rise
5. Nosing
6. Pitch

NOTE

The sum of twice the rise plus the going should be 550–700 mm/24" – 26" with an optimum of 600 mm/25".

Going/Run
The length of the step – excluding any overlap with other steps.

Open Riser
Stairs where there is no solid riser (or 'back') to the steps. The thread should overlap at least 16 mm (⅝") and the gap between treads should be less than 100 mm (4"). Prohibited in the US for public buildings.

Tread
The total length of one step.

Rise
The height of the step – measured from the surface of one step to the surface of the next.

Nosing
Projection of one step over another.

Pitch
The angle of the stairs relative to the horizontal – taken from the top line or nosing of the steps.

	Rise (mm)		Going (mm)		Pitch (mm)	
	Optimum	Maximum	Optimum	Minimum	Optimum	Maximum
Private	175	220	250	220	35	42
Semi-public	165	190	275	250	31	38
Public	150	180	300	280	27	33

NOTES

1. 'Private stairs' means stairs used by a limited number of people who are generally very familiar with the stairs, e.g. the internal stairs in a dwelling.
2. 'Semi-public stairs' means stairs used by larger numbers of people, some of whom may be unfamiliar with the stairs, e.g. in factories, offices, shops or common stairs serving more than one dwelling. In the US there is no distinction between public and semi-public.
3. 'Public stairs' means stairs used by large numbers of people at one time, e.g. in places of public assembly.
4. For stairs that are intended to satisfy the needs of ambulant disabled people, the rise should not be greater than 175mm / 7" and the going should not be less than 250mm/10".
5. In the US the rule of thumb for user comfort is: rise + run = 18" ±1" (2 × rise) + run = 25" ±1".

NB
Safety is a major concern in the design and construction of stairs. Parts B, K and M of the *Irish Technical Guidance Documents* on building regulations set out clear guidelines for stair design. Adherence to these guidelines ensures compliance with the building regulations. Standards will vary slightly from country to country. In the US follow the ADA Standards for Accessible Design.

3.2.4 **Setting Out a Staircase**

Example: Public building designed to metric standard in the British Isles

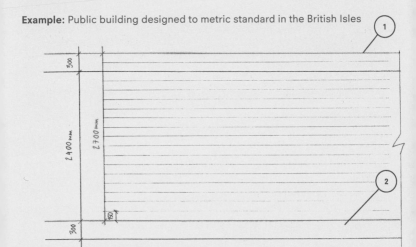

Step 1

Take the overall floor-to-floor height (e.g. including the thickness of the floor slab – in this case 2,700 mm) and divide by the required height of one step. In a public staircase, the optimum rise is 150 mm.

If the number of steps does not divide easily, round the height of the riser up or down to the nearest workable number, while staying within regulations. In this case, 150 mm divides easily into 2,700 mm, so draw horizontal parallel lines 150 mm apart.

Fig. 49

1. Upper floor slab
2. Ground floor slab

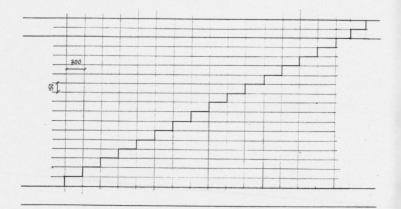

Step 2

Set out the dimensions of the stair goings (runs) – in this case 300 mm (optimum dimension for public stairs). Draw parallel vertical lines 300 mm apart.

NB

It's important that all risers and goings (runs) are consistent in a single flight of stairs – you can't make one step lower or shorter than the rest!

Step 3

Draw the profile of the stairs – in this case, there are 18 risers and 17 goings (runs).

There will always be one less going (run) than the number of risers on any stairs.

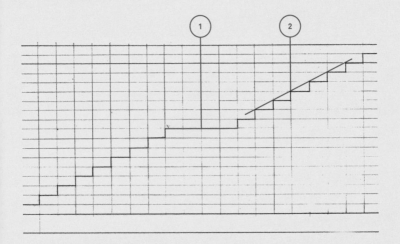

Figs 50 & 51

1. Landing
2. Pitch
3. Minimum headroom (2,000 mm)
4. Handrail height on stairs
   (840–900 mm)
5. Handrail height on landing
   (1,100 mm)

Step 4

The maximum number of risers in one flight of stairs is 16 in a private building and 12 in a public building. In this case, there are 18 risers, so we must include a landing.

The pitch is the angle of the line connecting the tops of the risers.

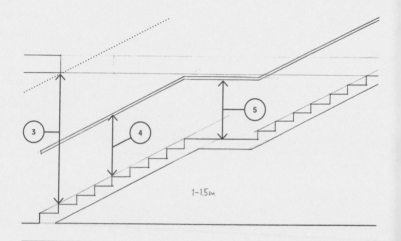

1–1.5m

NB

The landing should be at least as long as the stair width – for example, on stairs 1m wide the landing should be a minimum of 1 × 1m.

In a public building, the handrail should be 840–900mm vertically above, and parallel to, the pitch. On a landing, the handrail should be 1,100mm above the landing level. ADA Standards require handrails to be 34" to 38" above the leading edge of a stair tread, landing or ramp.

Step 5

The minimum headroom is 2m/6'-8" – measured vertically from the pitch of the stairs. This means the floor slab overhead must be cut back to this point.

The depth of the stair slab is determined by the material used. Steel, concrete, timber – all have different construction techniques and result in different depths.

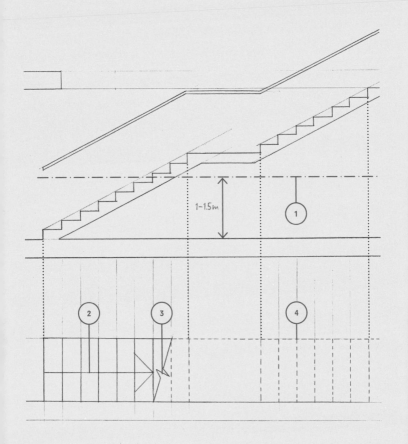

1–1.5 m

Step 6

Project the plan of the stairs from the section.

NB

Remember that a typical plan is cut 1 – 1.5 m (in the US about 4') above the floor level (shown left, as a 1 m high dash-dotted red line).

The minimum width of a private staircase is 800 mm (2'-7"). Public stairs are determined by fire regulations. As a rule of thumb, stairs should never be less than 900 mm when working in metric, or 3' when working in I-P.

Step 7

Indicate the cut line of stairs on a plan by using a break line – where the staircase is at the 1 – 1.5 m height above the floor level.

Use an arrow to show the direction of the stairs – the arrow always points towards the high point of the stairs.

Show with a broken line the continuation of the stairs above the cut line of the plan.

Fig. 52

1. Dash-dotted line – indicating the cut of the plan
2. Direction arrow
3. Break line
4. Broken line – indicating what goes on above the point at which the plan is cut

3.2.5 Multiple Flights of Stairs

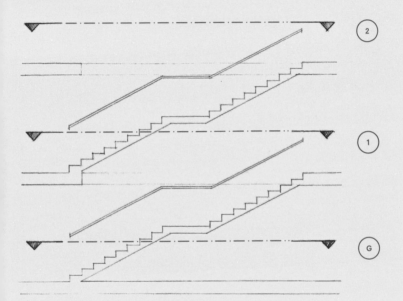

Figs 53 & 54

G. Ground floor

1. First floor

2. Second floor

Section

The red dash-dotted lines show where the plan level is cut on each floor.

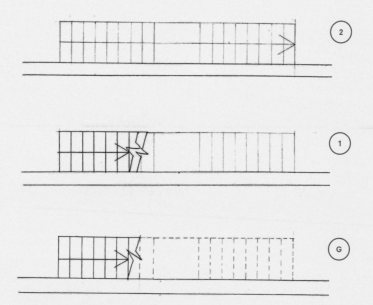

Plan

The ground-floor stairs are shown in plan up to the break line (1 – 1.5 m/ about 4' above floor level). Anything beyond this point is shown as a broken line. While the 1 – 1.5 m/4' cutting point is the convention, you can choose the height at which you draw your plan.

On the first floor-plan, both flights of stairs are shown: those coming up from the ground floor and those extending up to the second floor. They are separated by break lines at 1 – 1.5 m.

On the second-floor plan, the full plan of the stairs below is shown.

3.2.6 Shapes of Stairs

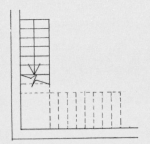

L-shaped Stairs

Stairs Around a Stairwell

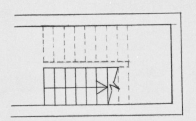

Dog-leg Stairs

3.2.7 Spiral & Helical Stairs

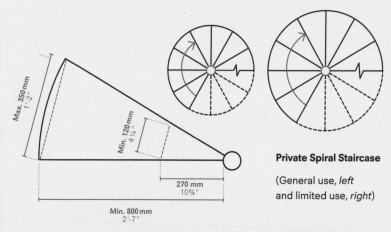

Private Spiral Staircase

(General use, *left* and limited use, *right*)

The setting out of spiral or helical stairs is governed by minimum and maximum goings, riser heights and stair clear widths, as in a straight flight of stairs. The difference with spiral stairs is that minimum and maximum goings apply to each step, but also relate to the clear width of the stairs as a whole.

The minimum going dimension on spiral stairs is measured 270 mm (10⅝") out from the inner face of the step or inner handrail, where one exists. This minimum going varies depending on the use of the stairs. For example, in a private

house the minimum going is 120 mm (4¼"), while for semi-public and public buildings it increases to 150 mm (6"). Note that spiral stairs are prohibited in public buildings in the US.

The diagram above shows the set out for a typical step for normal use in a private house.

The relationship between the rise (r) and the going (g) on spiral stairs should be: $480 \leq (2r + g) \geq 800$.

The minimum and maximum ranges for the rise and going are given in the table on the following page.

165

	Rise Per Tread	Min. Clear Width	Min. Going Centre
A	170–220 mm	600 mm	145 mm

Small private spiral staircase intended to be used by a limited number of people who are generally familiar with it, e.g. an internal staircase in a dwelling serving one room, not being a living room or kitchen; an access spiral staircase to a small room or plant in an office, shop or factory not used by the public; or a fire escape for a small number of people.

	Rise Per Tread	Min. Clear Width	Min. Going Centre
B	170–220 mm	800 mm	190 mm

Private spiral staircase similar to Category A, but also providing the main access to the upper floor of a private dwelling.

	Rise Per Tread	Min. Clear Width	Min. Going Centre
C	170–220 mm	800 mm	230 mm

Small semi-public spiral staircase intended to be used by a limited number of people, some of whom may be unfamiliar with it, e.g. a spiral staircase in a factory, office or shop or a common stair serving more than one dwelling.

	Rise Per Tread	Min. Clear Width	Min. Going Centre
D	150–190 mm	900 mm	250 mm

Semi-public spiral staircase intended to be used by larger numbers of people, some of whom may be unfamiliar with it, e.g. a spiral staircase in a factory, office or shop or a common stair serving more than one dwelling.

	Rise Per Tread	Min. Clear Width	Min. Going Centre
E	150–190 mm	1,000 mm	250 mm

Public spiral staircase intended to be used by large numbers of people at one time, e.g. a spiral staircase in a place of public assembly.

Sectional Elevation

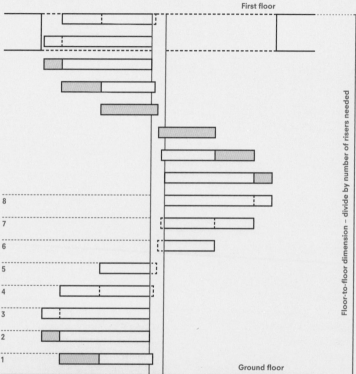

First floor

8

7

6

5

4

3

2

1

Ground floor

Floor-to-floor dimension – divide by number of risers needed

The plan of the stairs should be worked out according to the sizes required. The elevation and plan of the stairs combined allows you to work out the number of steps required from floor to floor and the clear head height.

The clear head height is 2 m/6'-8" as per a straight staircase.

The highest step may be in a different position on plan than the first step.

Risers are shown numbered.

3.2.8 Ramps

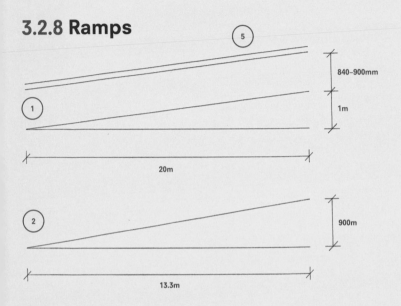

Figs 55 & 56

1. Standard ramp slope (1:20)
2. Short ramp (1:12)
3. Plan of ramp – uncut
4. Plan of ramp – cut at 300mm
5. Handrail

UK and Irish building standards indicate that a ramp should have a slope ratio of 1:20. This means that in order to rise 1m vertically, the ramp should be 20m in length (before the addition of any landings). For 1:20 ramps, landings are required every 12m.

For short ramps – where the rise is 900mm or less – a slope ratio of 1:12 is allowed, but landings are required every 4.5m.

The minimum width of a ramp in private dwellings is 800 mm. In public buildings, fire regulations determine the width of the ramp.

Handrails on a ramp should be 840–900 mm above and parallel to the line of the slope.

Public Buildings in the US follow the ADA Standards for Accessible Design which are slightly different from the values here. See **www. ada.gov** for more information.

On the plan of a ramp, always show the direction of the slope with an arrow – pointing towards the high point of the ramp. If the ramp is cut on the plan, use a break line (similar to the stairs, see Fig. 52).

Use a dashed line to indicate where the ramp continues on (above the cut line of the plan).

3.3
Windows & Doors

3.3.1 Terminology

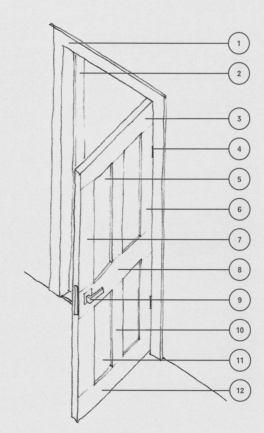

Fig. 57

1. Architrave
2. Door frame
3. Top rail
4. Hinge
5. Door leaf
6. Hanging/hinge stile
7. Closing/latch stile
8. Middle/locking rail
9. Door handle
10. Muntin
11. Recessed panel
12. Bottom rail

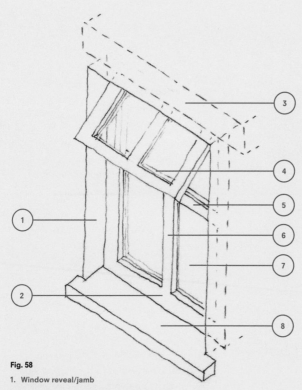

Fig. 58

1. Window reveal/jamb
2. Frame
3. Lintel
4. Opening casement
5. Transom
6. Mullion
7. Fixed Light
8. Window cill (sill)

3.3.2 Types of Windows

Fixed Light
No opening section. This is a single pane of glass attached to a frame.

Casement Window
Windows with an opening section are sometimes called 'casement windows'.

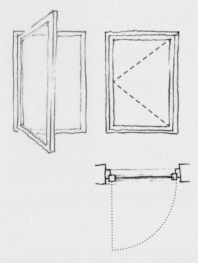

Side-hung Window
The opening section is hinged on one side – typically it opens outwards. Make a dashed line arrow pointing to the hinged side of the opening. Scandinavian and German convention is the reverse – with the arrow pointing away from the hinge.

Always indicate the open position and swing of the window on the plan with a dotted line.

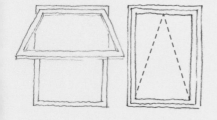

Top-hung Window

The opening section is hinged at the top – typically it opens outwards. Make a dashed line arrow pointing to the hinged side of the opening – in this case the hinges are at the top.

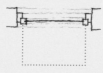

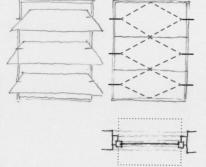

Louvred Window

The window is hinged at the horizontal centres of the glass panes. This type of window is difficult to thermally seal, so it is now rarely used.

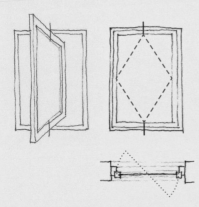

Vertical Pivot Window
The window is hinged
at the horizontal centre.

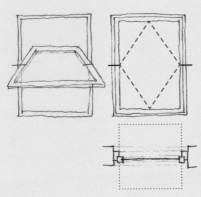

Horizontal Pivot Window
The window is hinged
at the vertical centre.

Sliding Sash/Casement Window
These windows are not hinged, but slide up or down (vertically or horizontally). Arrows are used to indicate the direction of any moving parts.

3.3.3 Types of Doors

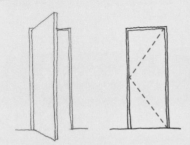

Side-hung Door (Single)
This is the simplest door
type and is widely used.

Indicate on the plan with a dotted
line the open position and swing of
the door. This can be shown using
a straight line or a quadrant.

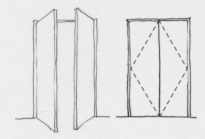

Side-hung Door (Double)

In this case, the hinges are on both sides of the frame. These doors can swing in one or two directions.

TIP

Think about the position of the door frame within the opening – the door could be flush with the internal or external face of the wall or centrally placed. This can have significant design implications.

Door and window openings seen deep within the wall emphasize the thickness of the wall and its mass. Frames that are flush with the façade emphasize the planar quality of the wall.

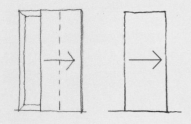

Sliding Door (Single)

A sliding door can be hung on a rail at the top or slide on a track in the ground (usually recessed into the ground) or both.

If a guide rail is fixed to the ground, it should be shown on the plan.

Indicate with a small arrow on plans and elevations the direction that the door slides.

The door can slide on the external face of the wall or within a recess built into the wall. In the case of the latter, the leaf is not visible when the door is open. This is sometimes known as a pocket door.

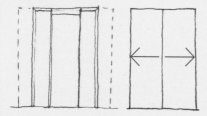

Sliding Door (Double)

Double sliding doors can be hung on a rail at the top or slide on a track in the ground (usually recessed into the ground) or both.

If a guide rail is fixed to the ground, it should be shown on the plan.

Indicate with a small arrow on plans and elevations the directions in which the doors slide.

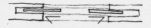

The doors can slide on the external face of the wall or within a recess built into the wall. In the case of the latter, the leaves are not visible when the doors are open.

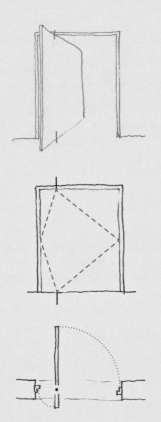

Pivot Door

A pivot door can be set with a central or offset pivot hinge. In general, these are used for large openings as there is a smaller 'clear width' than with a simple hinge door.

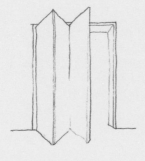

Folding Door

There are many variations on the folding door. Depending on the width of the opening, you can set the number and widths of the door leaves.

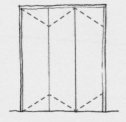

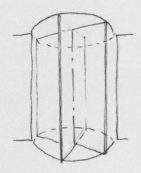

Revolving Door
Usually used in public or large commercial buildings. They can be difficult to negotiate for disabled users.

There are various formations of revolving door – they may contain two, three or four compartments.

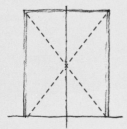

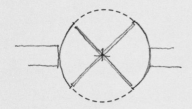

3.3.4 Drawing Doors and Windows at Various Scales

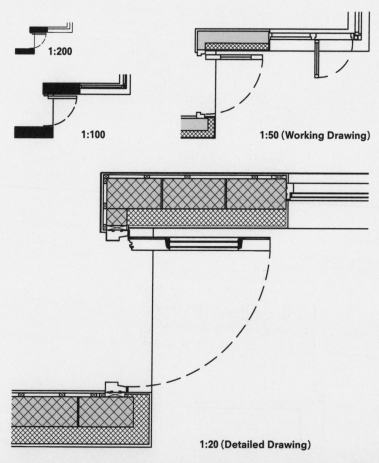

1:200

1:100

1:50 (Working Drawing)

1:20 (Detailed Drawing)

3.3.5 Side-hung Casement Window in Plan and Section

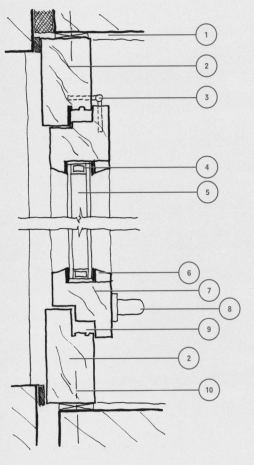

1:2 (Plan)

Fig. 59

1. Plaster
2. Frame
3. Hinge
4. Rubber gasket
5. Double glazing
6. Glazing bead
7. Opening sash
8. Handle
9. Weather stripping
10. Screw fixing

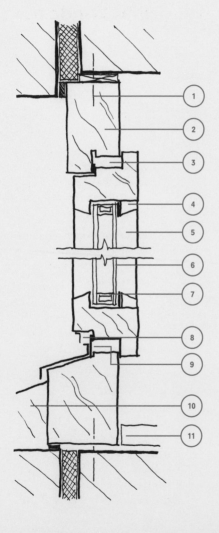

1:2 (Section)

Fig. 60

1. Screw fixing
2. Frame
3. Stepped rebate
4. Glazing bead
5. Opening sash
6. Double glazing
7. Rubber gasket
8. Rainwater drainage channel
9. Weather bar
10. External window cill (sill)
11. Internal window cill (sill)

3.3.6 Setting Out Doors and Windows

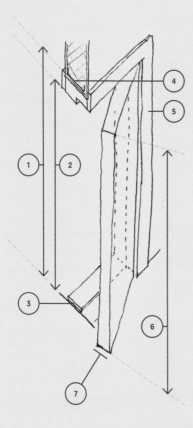

Section

Take care when drawing and annotating doors that the critical dimensions are included.

'Structural opening' refers to the dimension between the finished floor level and the underside of the lintel. This is a critical dimension for setting out on site.

The 'clear vertical height' refers to the dimension between the underside of the door frame and the door saddle.

NB

The door leaf height, width and thickness will be needed by the door manufacturer.

Fig. 61

1. Structural opening
2. Clear vertical height
3. Door saddle/threshold
4. Lintel
5. Architrave
6. Door leaf height
7. Door leaf thickness

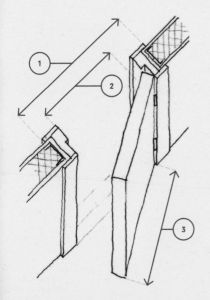

Plan

In plan, 'structural opening' refers to the dimension of the gap in the wall – before any door frame has been added.

'Clear opening' refers to the inner dimension of the door frame less the thickness of the door leaf – e.g. the usable width of the open door. Remember to exclude the thickness of the door leaf.

Fig. 62

1. Structural opening
2. Clear opening
3. Door leaf width

3.4
Hatching & Lettering

3.4.1 Hatching

Hatching is used in working drawings to indicate types of materials when you cut through them in plan or section. The patterns allow you to distinguish one material from another on your drawings and also allow you to read other people's technical drawings – even if the legend is in another language. Slight variations do occur, however, in international hatching standards so confirm local conventions and be sure to provide a legend. Hatching is generally used on construction/working drawings at scales from 1:100 to 1:1. It is not generally used on presentation or schematic drawings. Hatching is done with a fine light line so as not to dominate the drawing – a 2H or 4H lead weight is appropriate.

Large Scale
i.e. 1:2 / 1:5 / 1:10

Small Scale
i.e. 1:20 / 1:50 / 1:100

Brickwork

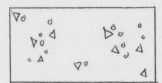

Concrete

Large Scale
i.e. 1:2 / 1:5 / 1:10

Small Scale
i.e. 1:20 / 1:50 / 1:100

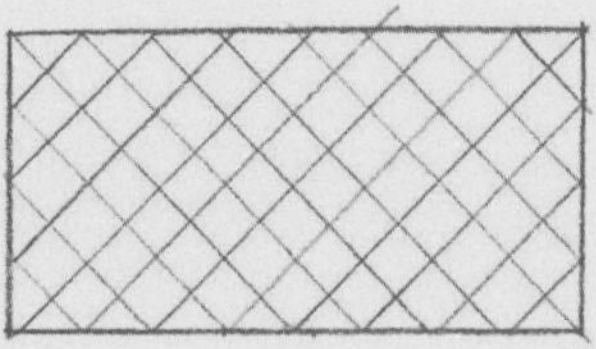

Blockwork
Option 1

(More commonly used
in continental Europe.
Also used to denote
rigid insulation.)

Blockwork
Option 2

(More commonly
used in the UK
and Ireland.)

Earth

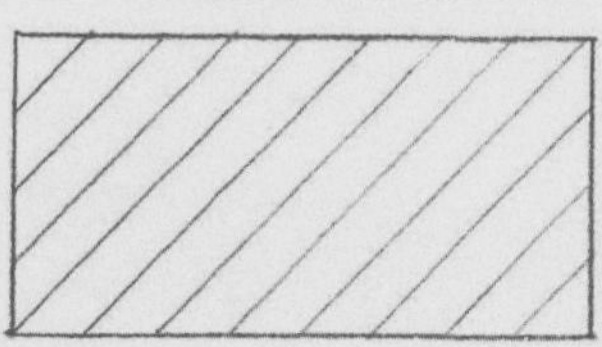

Steel

193

Large Scale

i.e. 1:2 / 1:5 / 1:10

Small Scale

i.e. 1:20 / 1:50 / 1:100

**Wrought
Timber**

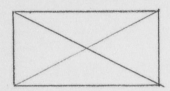

**Unwrought
Timber**

The term **wrought timber** describes timber that has been planed or finished. It is generally used for joinery. **Unwrought timber** refers to unfinished timber usually used for joists, studs and other structural elements.

The sizing of timber elements is important to get right, as the dimensions for wrought timber are smaller than those of unwrought timber because of the finishing process.

See **Sections 6.3.11** and **6.3.12**.

Large Scale
i.e. 1:2 / 1:5 / 1:10

Small Scale
i.e. 1:20 / 1:50 / 1:100

Insulation
(typically fibre-glass)

(Rigid insulation is sometimes shown as a hatch pattern similar to Blockwork Option 1.)

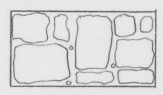

Insulation
(Germany and Switzerland)

Hardcore

Plaster/Screed

195

Large Scale

i.e. 1:2 / 1:5 / 1:10

Small Scale

i.e. 1:20 / 1:50 / 1:100

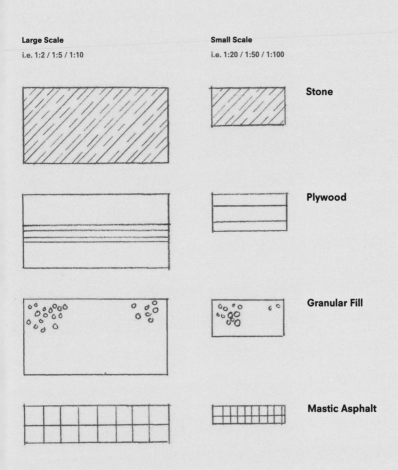

Stone

Plywood

Granular Fill

Mastic Asphalt

Large Scale

i.e. 1:2 / 1:5 / 1:10

Small Scale

i.e. 1:20 / 1:50 / 1:100

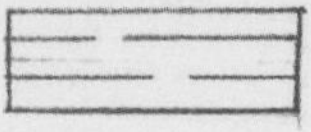

Glass

NB
It is rare to hatch
materials in elevation –
glass is the exception.

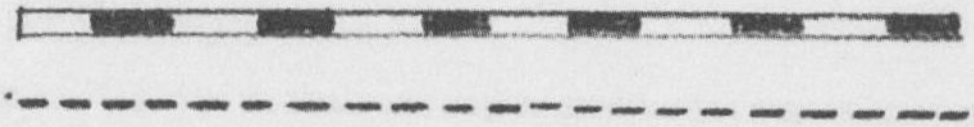

**Damp-proof
Course/
Damp-proof
Membrane
(DPC/DPM)**

3.4.2 Lettering

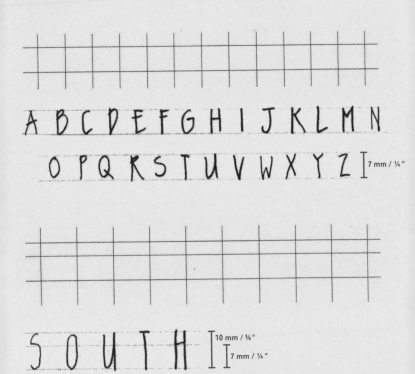

A B C D E F G H I J K L M N

O P Q R S T U V W X Y Z 7 mm / ¼ "

S O U T H I 10 mm / ⅜ " 7 mm / ¼ "

18MM TONGUED & GROOVED
HARDWOOD FLOOR-BOARDS

100MM KINGSPAN SOLID
INSULATION (TO ARCH.'S
SPEC.)

DONT SQUASH THE LETTERS

OR

S P R E A D   T O O   F A R

The first principle of all lettering is legibility. Set up very faint guidelines before starting to write. Write in thin monoline lettering – i.e. without showing thickness to the characters.

The size of the lettering should relate to the overall impact needed – i.e. main titles should be larger than notes.

Group all text in a neat column alongside the drawing. Use reference lines to connect the notes to the drawing.

Avoid cramping the text or spreading it out so much that it becomes difficult to read.

Lettering takes practice. It is worth putting the time in, as neat and clear lettering greatly enhances an architectural drawing.

4

Working Through Drawing

Drawing survives and even thrives in this digital age because – simply put – there is no better process for exploring and expressing visual ideas with the directness, personal expressiveness, or inventive specificity that drawing provides. It is the visual mind's best, fastest and most flexible way of thinking.
—Christopher Brown

Architects use drawing processes to differing ends depending on the focus of their work at any one time. Drawing is a means of communicating ideas, but it is also a process through which ideas are explored. The inexplicable connection between hand, eye and brain that occurs when we draw is key to the generation of thought on paper. This connection can also be referred to as kinaesthetic learning, or learning by doing. 'Drawing is thinking' – it is not just the end product; rather, the process of drawing brings up questions that when answered guide us in the design process.

In this chapter we look at the range of drawing types commonly used by architectural students and architects in practice to both explore and represent ideas at the various stages of the design process.

We also look at a sample project in which a number of drawing types were used in the design process to develop, as well as to explain and represent, the project.

4.1
Drawing
to Observe
& Record

4.1.1 Drawing From Observation

Drawing from observation – whether it is life drawing, still life, small objects or buildings – is good practice when it comes to honing your drawing and sketching skills. It is true to say that drawing ability improves with repetition and practice.

Another benefit of drawing from observation is that it will develop your feeling for form, a core sense for an architect.

Sketch books are ideal when drawing on your travels or for jotting down and recording ideas.

The following series of drawings and sketches illustrate some of the many types used by architects and students.

In the drawing opposite, a Rapidograph ink drafting pen is sketched using a combination of lead pencil, colouring pencil and watercolour at different scales.

We recommend that you practise drawing and sketching in different media on a regular basis.

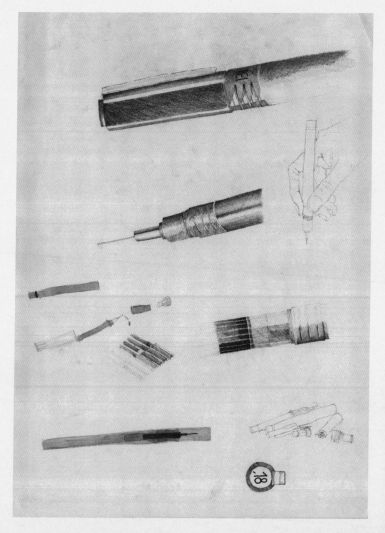

4.1.2 Object Study

Drawing at different speeds and in different media is a good way to develop intuitive drawing skills.

The sketch below is a 30-second drawing of a garlic press in soft pencil, completed without lifting the pencil. Opposite is a 30-minute sketch of the same garlic press using a graphite pencil.

This object study of a garlic press concludes with the compilation of a hard-line drawing. The drawing is set out with plan, sections and elevations, all aligned with each other.

However, this drawing goes one step further – by demonstrating how the object moves, showing its different positions in dotted line. The thickness of the metal handle of the garlic press is also indicated.

The number of sections indicates the changing profile of the handle.

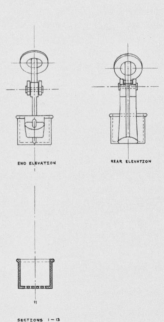

END ELEVATION

REAR ELEVATION

SECTIONS 1 – 13

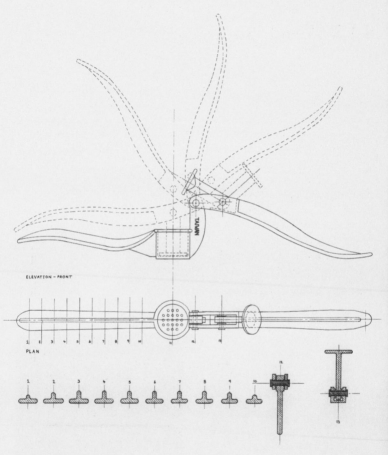

ELEVATION – FRONT

PLAN

James Dolan Prize Drawing

4.1.3 Sketch Books

Architects use sketch books to record a range of information. Quick analytical drawings can be a useful way of understanding the proportions and forms of buildings you visit. Try to imagine what the plan of the room you are in would look like and what a section would be. These analytical drawings take practice, but making them is an invaluable skill for understanding the buildings around you.

Over the next few pages, we show a range of architects' sketches from sketch books.

Fig. 63
Analytical sketch of Sir
John Soane's Dulwich
Picture Gallery

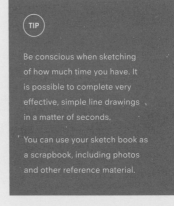

TIP

Be conscious when sketching of how much time you have. It is possible to complete very effective, simple line drawings in a matter of seconds.

You can use your sketch book as a scrapbook, including photos and other reference material.

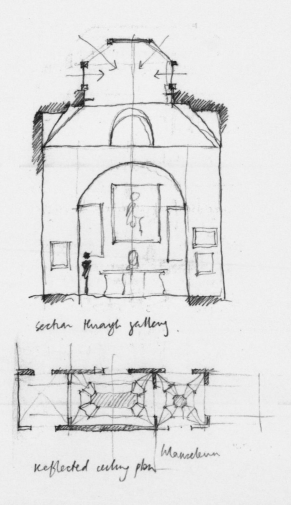

section through gallery.

reflected ceiling plan   Mausoleum

Fig. 64

Sketch proposals

Think more like Arctic or lunar science base than urban laboratory. Duties.

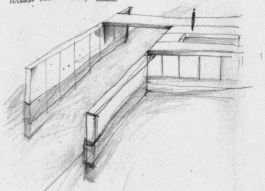

Why bother with a courtyard when u can use the roof as an outdoor eating / relaxing space — needs some shelter — too exposed

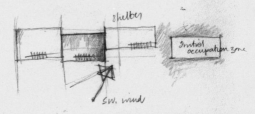

shelter

Initial occupation zone

s.w. wind

Fig. 65
Photo of materials study

Stained wall, Blackrock Baths.

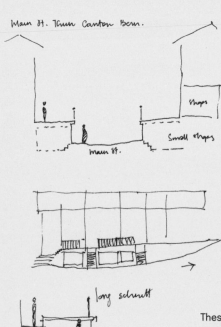

Main St. Thun Canton Bern.

shops

Small shops

Main st.

long schnitt

stairs section

Fig. 66

Quick analytical sketches

These sketches show it is possible to complete informative drawings in very little time. In this case, the architect wanted to note the unusual stepped street section, so details such as windows and doors were not included. With a minimum of detail, these simple drawings capture a specific point clearly and economically.

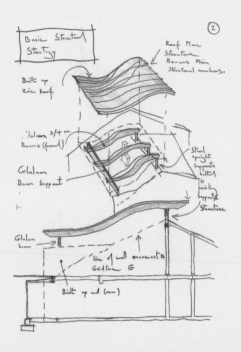

Fig. 67

Structural strategy sketch

Sketch books are useful for jotting down ideas and notes. The sketch above records the elements involved in a idea about an exposed structure at an early design stage, which was developed and altered as the project evolved.

The drawing opposite shows a section through a small cottage. The sketch includes dimensions and elements such as furniture, windows and doors, and details of construction are carefully noted. This type of drawing could be used as a template for drawing up a survey – see **Chapter 5**.

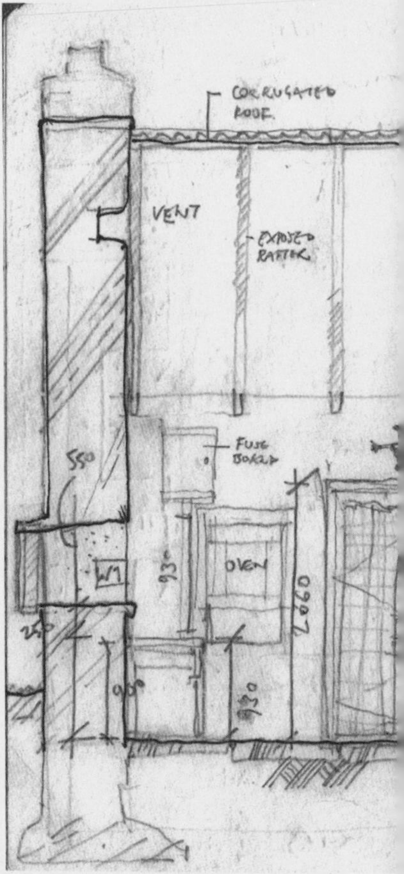

Fig. 68
Bothar Buí by architect Robin Walker.
Sketch courtesy of Dermot Boyd

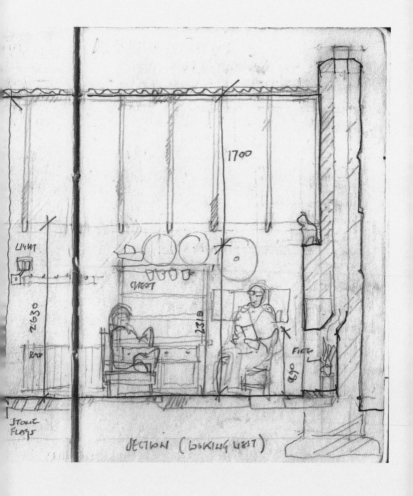

SECTION (LOOKING WEST)

Fig. 69
Igualada Cemetery by Enric
Miralles and Carme Pinos.
Sketch courtesy of Michael Pike

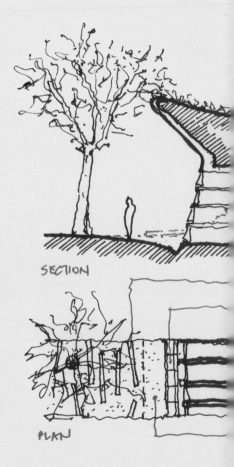

SECTION

PLAN

NB
By including a proportional plan,
section and elevation in the same
sketch, a more complete record
can be achieved.

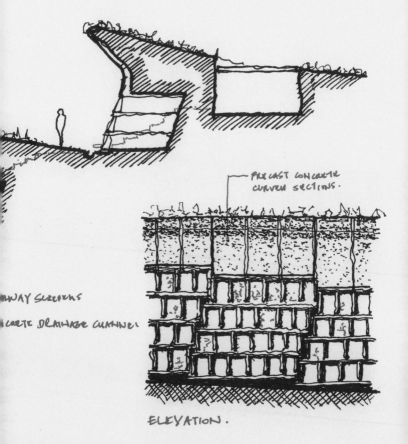

PRECAST CONCRETE
CURVED SECTIONS.

RWAY SLEEPERS

CRETE DRAINAGE CHANNEL

ELEVATION.

OH WASHED CONCRETE WITH ROUNDED PEBBLES

Fig. 70
Igualada Cemetery by Enric Miralles
and Carme Pinos.
Sketch courtesy of Gerry Cahill

NB
A pictorial approach to
recording information can
capture the spirit of a place.

4.2
Representing the Idea

Drawing, as a way of thinking and developing ideas, is a fundamental process in design. When it comes to communicating a developed design concept, different drawing types are required that will visually communicate that concept clearly and succinctly in a single image or a sequence of images. The most relevant type of drawing can depend on who the audience is; for example, a drawing for a building contractor will require different kinds of information than a drawing for a client. Often the audience is yourself; you draw to clarify your own intentions. This can be done in numerous ways. In this section we show you a small selection of the many ways in which ideas can be represented in drawing form. In each case, a description is given of the method and materials used.

4.2.1 **Trace from Photographs**

Method

A number of photographs were taken from a height to capture the view of a city block in Dublin. In this instance, they were taken from the top of a crane on an adjacent site. These photos were then put together to give the overall view.

It is also possible to access this type of view by using Bing Maps at www.bing.com/maps or Google Maps at www.google.com/maps.

An A1-sized sheet of tracing paper was then overlaid on the photos and the image was traced. This involved a certain amount of artistic interpretation, because all the detail on the photos cannot end up on the final sheet.

Coloured paper was fixed to the back of the sheet to highlight different elements: two sites either side of the railway track, the railway track itself and a community building in the background.

Purpose

The purpose of this drawing was to represent the relevant areas of interest relating to a thesis proposal.

Fig. 71

Site photo-montage and a tracing

4.2.2 Drawing Sequence

There are a number of ways to represent a project spatially in two dimensions. The following sequence of sketches do this. They have been made by overlaying photographs.

The series of images progress towards the proposed project, in this case a theatre.

Location
Capel Street, Dublin

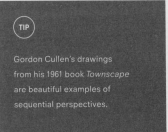

TIP

Gordon Cullen's drawings from his 1961 book *Townscape* are beautiful examples of sequential perspectives.

Dots on the plan indicate the route taken in this sequence of sketches.

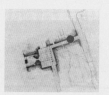

4.2.3 Exploded Axonometric

An exploded axonometric drawing shows the main elements of a design separated out from each other but related back to their original relationship spatially, usually with dotted lines.

There is skill involved in deciding which elements to extrude and where to place them on the sheet.

In this example, colour has been used to highlight different elements such as structure, furniture and cladding.

NB
See how to set up and draw an 'axo' (axonometric view) in **Section 2.3.3**.

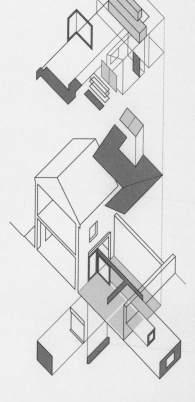

Fig. 72
Drawing courtesy of Killian Doherty,
Architectural Field Office

4.2.4 Rotated Plan/Part-isometric View

Depending on the complexity of a
design, it may be helpful to explain
it by using this approach.

Plans are laid out in sequence,
but they are rotated through 30°.
In order to understand the context,
sometimes it can be useful to
show selected parts of the design
in three dimensions while relating
them to the plan.

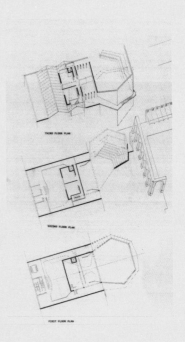

4.2.5 Sketch Perspective and Photograph Overlay

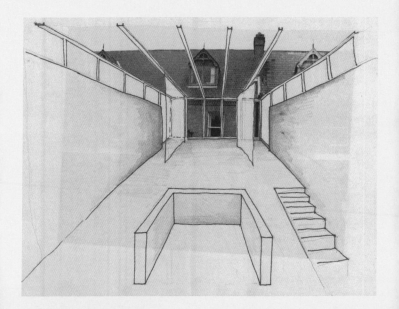

This is a method of inserting a sketch into a photograph to represent an idea quickly. This is often used to put your proposal in context. A photo of the site can be inserted behind a sketch of your proposal.

NB
See how to set up and draw a sketch perspective in **Chapter 2**.

4.2.6 Adding Depth

This drawing represents a proposed school in plan and in its urban context. The digital drawing was printed in black and white, and the site detail was added in pencil.

It was also necessary to highlight the proposed urban-scale intervention, which involved more subtle changes to the urban landscape. The type and extent of these changes were highlighted by the use of colouring pencil applied to the printed sheet by hand, using tone to create a sense of depth and shadow, and delineating the relevant area to be altered.

Shading and texture give a richness to the surrounding context of the building.

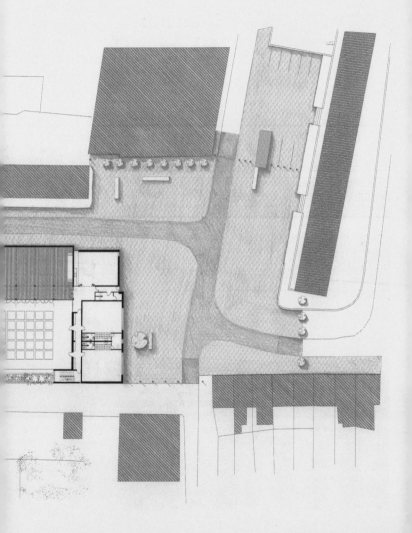

4.2.7 Watercolour Sketches

Orthographic representations describe your project in an understandable two-dimensional format. But they lack the third dimension that helps the viewer imagine the project and communicates the spirit of the architect's intentions.

Three-dimensional sketches and perspectives are a very useful way of explaining your proposals to people who do not understand orthographic representation. They also help you to visualize your own proposals.

Method

Draw a perspective view on watercolour paper (either hard-line or freehand, depending on your level of ability – see **Section 2.4**).

Use watercolour washes to develop the image. When the watercolour has dried, you can use graphite pencil to show shadow.

Fig. 73

Sketch of external walkway

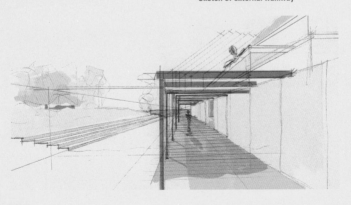

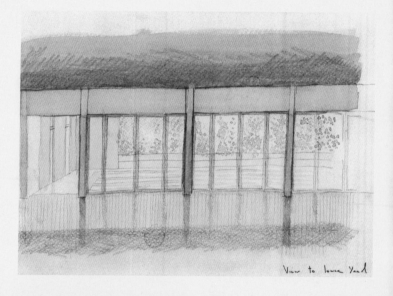

View to lower Yard

Fig. 74

View from inside to outside

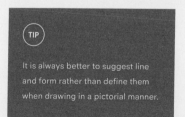

TIP

It is always better to suggest line and form rather than define them when drawing in a pictorial manner.

235

4.2.8 Adding Depth in Section

CROSS SECTION

Achieving tone and depth and a sense of materiality is an acquired skill which you develop by doing. The drawing above is a great example of the use of graphite and coloured pencil, to this effect.

Fig. 75

Adding depth in section

– Conor Maguire

4.2.9 **Scenography**

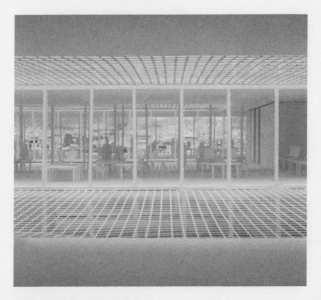

Scenography in architecture involves the creation of a physical model and photographing it, to convey an atmosphere or vision for the idea behind the project.

Fig. 76

Plaza De Les Glories Catalanes, Conor McGowan et al

4.2.10 SketchUp/Photoshop

Using the software SketchUp to model a building at the early design stage is a very quick and accessible method of developing three-dimensional images in perspective; 2D images can be extracted from SketchUp as jpegs. The image above was then brought into Photoshop and rendered using material images, layers and levels of transparency.

Fig. 77

SketchUp model image, rendered in Photoshop. Image courtesy of Gorman Architects/Sean Lynch

4.2.11 **3D Digital Image**

3D digital images are produced in a number of ways using CAD software to make three-dimensional models. By extracting a two-dimensional isometric or perspective view like the image above, 2D views can then be rendered in Photoshop to add materials and a sense of light and tone – or this aspect can be developed in the 3D model itself to achieve a photorealistic image, depending on the software used.

Fig. 78

Glasnevin 1916 Centenary Chapel, Emer O'Daly, O'Daly Architects

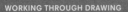

4.3
Drawings
in Sequence

Here we look at the sequence of drawings that an architect might use to design, develop and explain a project.

The Precast Concrete House in Howth, by FKL Architects, was completed in 2009, following a five-year design and construction period. FKL Architects stress the importance of designing from first principles, and they often rely on a 'concept sketch' as a way of defining and informing the design process. This concept comes out of site and brief analysis. FKL began this project by making models of the site and sketching possible configurations. You can see in these notebook sketches that this project evolved through a series of sections and three-dimensional drawings. In the early stages of the design process, you should use your notebook often, and make concept models and drawings of your site.

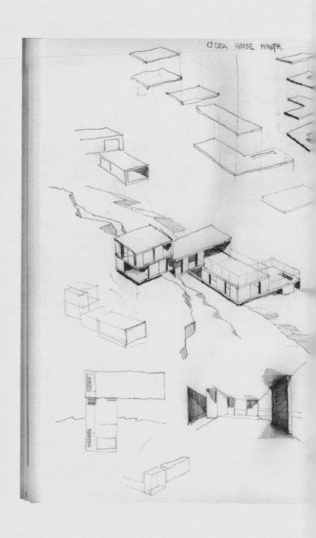

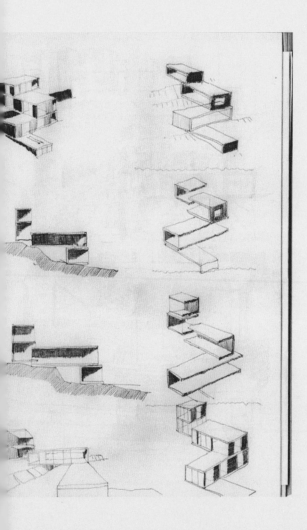

Early sketch ideas
Drawings of the
Precast Concrete
House in Howth,
County Dublin

4.3.1 Early Site Model

Making site models allows you to understand the possibilities and limitations of slope, scale and topography. Site models at an early stage of a project allow you to place proposals 'on site'.

In this project, the site sloped steeply to the sea and was divided lengthways by a deep natural gulley. Making the model allowed the architects to fully appreciate and explore the options in terms of orientation and positioning.

4.3.2 **Concept Sketch**

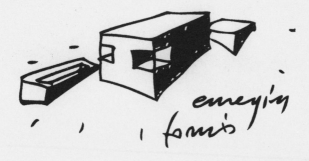

emerging forms

Having worked through site analysis and early design attempts, FKL then developed a concept sketch. The project is drawn here as three forms: the swimming pool, the house and the garage, each set at different heights. These three forms slip past one another as they move down the site towards the sea.

This concept sketch became a touchstone throughout the detailed design of the project.

4.3.3 Working Models

As the project developed, FKL continued to make models, at a larger scale, examining options for composition and façades. These models were made as working models – i.e. they were photographed, altered and made to work as tools of the design process rather than as final presentation models.

At the same time as making physical models, FKL were working with digital models and collage. Making 3D drawings of the project and collaging-in photographs of the site allowed the architects and clients to imagine how the proposals would look at eye level in context.

You can achieve this quite easily by constructing one-point perspective drawings of your proposal and using photographs of your site as a background (see **Section 4.2.5**).

See **Section 2.4** for instructions on constructing one-point perspectives.

4.3.4 Working Drawings

When the building had been designed and was ready for construction, tender drawings were prepared. These are detailed drawings at a range of scales to show materials, dimensions and construction.

Tender drawings (bid documents in the US) are working drawings and are issued to contractors to obtain quotes for construction, so it is critical that they contain all relevant information – including dimensions and descriptions of the materials. Tender/working drawings typically consist of GA (general arrangement) drawings showing the layout of the building in plan, section and elevation, with detailed drawings at 1:50, 1:20, 1:10 and sometimes 1:5 or 1:2.

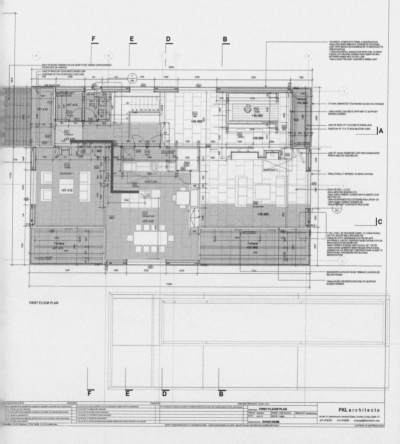

FIRST FLOOR PLAN

FKL architects

This is a part of the 1:50 tender-stage plan.

The drawing shows setting-out dimensions, section lines and floor levels, as well as written notes explaining construction.

The notes are carefully placed to the right of the drawing for clarity and describe the build-up of the construction. The contractor uses these notes to price work, to order materials and to build from. These are complex drawings and are dense with information.

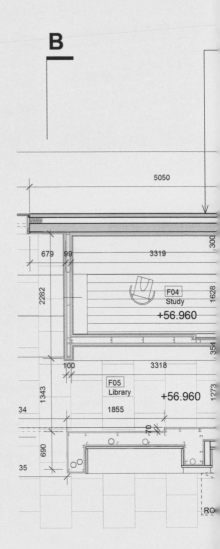

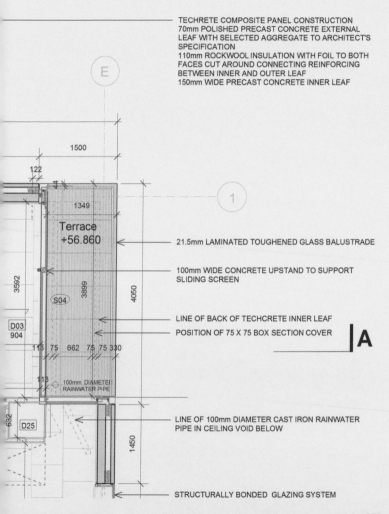

TECHRETE COMPOSITE PANEL CONSTRUCTION
70mm POLISHED PRECAST CONCRETE EXTERNAL
LEAF WITH SELECTED AGGREGATE TO ARCHITECT'S
SPECIFICATION
110mm ROCKWOOL INSULATION WITH FOIL TO BOTH
FACES CUT AROUND CONNECTING REINFORCING
BETWEEN INNER AND OUTER LEAF
150mm WIDE PRECAST CONCRETE INNER LEAF

E

1500

122

1349

Terrace
+56.860

21.5mm LAMINATED TOUGHENED GLASS BALUSTRADE

100mm WIDE CONCRETE UPSTAND TO SUPPORT
SLIDING SCREEN

3592

3899

4050

1

S04

LINE OF BACK OF TECHCRETE INNER LEAF

D03
904

POSITION OF 75 X 75 BOX SECTION COVER

113 75   662   75 75 330

A

113

100mm DIAMETER
RAINWATER PIPE

682

LINE OF 100mm DIAMETER CAST IRON RAINWATER
PIPE IN CEILING VOID BELOW

D25

1450

STRUCTURALLY BONDED GLAZING SYSTEM

4.3.5 Site Sketches

This sketch is typical of the kind of drawing you may do on site while the building is under construction. Issues often arise during the construction of a project that can be resolved with a quick hand drawing, which helps the architect communicate with the contractor.

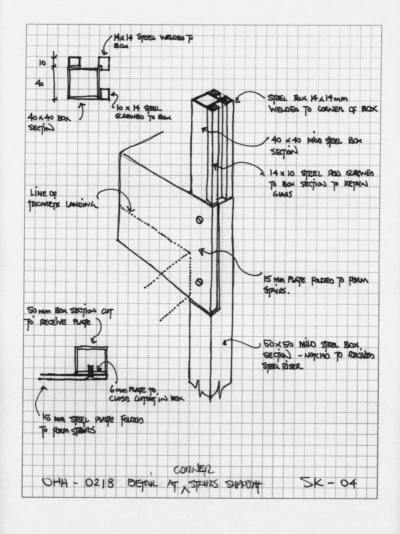

14 x 14 STEEL WELDED TO BOX

10 x 14 STEEL SCREWED TO BOX

40 x 40 BOX SECTION

10

40

STEEL BOX 14 x 14mm WELDED TO CORNER OF BOX

40 x 40 MILD STEEL BOX SECTION

14 x 10 STEEL ROD SCREWED TO BOX SECTION TO RETAIN GLASS

LINE OF TECHCRETE LANDING

15 mm PLATE FOLDED TO FORM STAIRS.

50 mm BOX SECTION CUT TO RECEIVE PLATE

6 mm PLATE TO CLOSE CUTOUT IN BOX

15 mm STEEL PLATE FOLDED TO FORM STAIRS

50 x 50 MILD STEEL BOX SECTION - NOTCHED TO RECEIVE STEEL RISER

CORNER

OHH - 0218   DETAIL AT STAIRS SUPPORT   SK - 04

4.3.6 Presentation Drawings

When the construction of the building was complete, FKL then remade their detailed working drawings as presentation drawings. The presentation drawings were used to publicize the project.

This process eliminates much of the technical information (e.g. hatching, dimensions and shading) from the working drawings and allows them to be understood more easily.

You will follow a similar process when you prepare presentation drawings for reviews. Take care to show the difference between walls and openings, and to make the drawings as clear and legible as possible. Your audience is key. To illustrate the spatial organization of the building, a simplified presentation drawing is more suitable than a dense 'working drawing'.

Building under construction

Completed building

1   5

First Floor Plan

Presentation plan

Drawings and images courtesy of FKL Architects

255

4.4
Working Through Models

Architects use scale models as a key part of design decision-making and presentation. Examples vary widely from quick sketch models to complex and detailed large-scale models. In this section we'll show you some examples of architectural models, explaining when they may be useful and giving you tips on making models by hand. While some models are time-consuming and laborious, others can be made quickly and efficiently. It's worth pausing before you begin to clarify exactly what you want the model to show or test. Try out a wide range of techniques and materials – card, plaster casting, wood, foam, metal – and you will find ways of working that suit you and your personal architectural interests.

4.4.1 **Sketch Models**

Making early sketch models before you've 'fixed' your design can be a very helpful way of testing your ideas. They can open up possibilities that are difficult to develop in two-dimensional hard-line drawings. Sketch models are ideal for testing a number of iterations quickly. They are also useful for testing the scale, proportion and spatial arrangement of your proposals. Sketch models are most effective for judging how the spaces of your design work, rather than on what the building will look like. They can be made simply from lightweight card, watercolour or cartridge paper. Try scoring and folding lightweight card rather than gluing pieces together to make quick models.

Fig. 79

Paper sketch model of University Campus UTEC Lima, Peru, Grafton Architects

4.4.2 **Contour Models**

Contour models show the topography of a site in a series of layered contours. They can be made by hand using sheets of card or thin layers of foam or wood. Each layer corresponds to one contour line on a map (a contour line is a line connecting points of the same height). Critical to the usefulness of a contour map is judging the best increments for the contours. If you are working at a relatively large scale (for example 1:2,000 or 1:5,000) you may decide to use 5m (16') as the increment between contour lines, whereas for a larger-scale model you may decide to set the contours at .5m (1'-8") or less.

Fig. 80

Contour site model, Boyd Cody Architects

TIP

Always check that the contours correspond to the thickness of the card. If you are making a 1:1,000 model and showing contours at 2m intervals, your card thickness should be 2mm.

4.4.3 Site Models

Positioning your proposal on a scale model of the site allows you make judgements about the form and massing of your design. Site models of urban areas may include the surrounding buildings, roads and boundaries; site models in rural areas could be contour models, which may include planting, boundaries and natural features. The scale of the site model you make should be determined by what stage of the process you are at, and the level of detail you wish to test. Site models can be made from card or other sheet materials, or could be cast.

Fig. 81
Site model, Architecture Technology
Students, TUDublin

4.4.4 Structural Models

Models are a great tool to work out the structural elements of your designs. Try to use materials that accurately recreate the structural materials or elements you are testing, for example balsa-wood sticks are good for frame structures, whereas plaster casts can create a good approximation of cast in-situ concrete.

Fig. 82
Structural model, plaster-cast study for a student community centre project

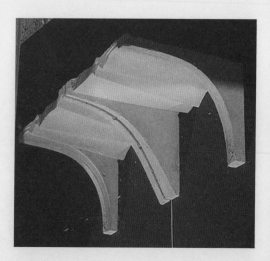

4.4.5 Precedent Models

In your study of architecture you will often be asked to study seminal buildings (or 'precedents'). In trying to understand these buildings, making a scale model can be an invaluable path to understanding the spatial qualities that make these buildings significant.

The complexity and scale of the precedent model you make depends on what is particularly significant about the building. It could be the relationship to the site, the spatial organization or the structural system used.

Fig. 83

Precedent model,

Barcelona Pavilion,

Mies van der Rohe

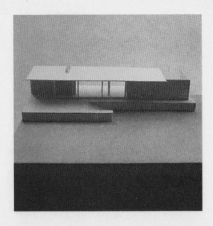

4.4.6 SketchUp Models

SketchUp is a digital modelling programme which can be employed to make quick three-dimensional models. While SketchUp is relatively straightforward to use, and can be a useful tool in developing your designs, we recommend making physical scale models as a primary design tool.

Fig. 84

SketchUp model

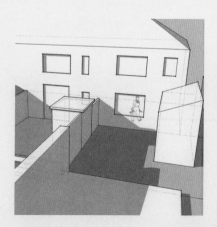

4.4.7 Interior Models

Large-scale interior models (1:50, 1:20 or even 1:10 / in the US: ¼ ", ½ ", or 1" = 1'-0") are great for making accurate judgements about the proportions of, and light in, the internal spaces of your project. They could include furniture and accurate representations of the materials and finishes you propose. Plan in advance the key view you wish to capture so that this wall of your model is removable (in order to take photos).

What these models look like on the outside is generally unimportant – use tape and sewing pins to fix walls, which you can then adapt and move. Interior models are ideal for photographing and then collaging-in exterior details. They are useful both as part of your design process and also as presentation tool.

TIP

Take your model outside to photograph it in daylight. Position it so that it aligns with the site's orientation to accurately recreate the quality of light at various times of the day.

Fig. 85

Large-scale façade and interior study model,

Boyd Cody Architects

4.4.8 Presentation Models

In preparation for reviews of your design project you may wish to make a final or presentation model. This can be used to explain your project to your tutors or peers. As with any scale model, the model is an abstraction of your design – you cannot represent every detail of your design, so before planning your presentation model you should clarify what are the key ideas in your project that you wish to discuss. This should direct the kind of presentation model you wish to make.

Fig. 86

Presentation model, Boyd Cody Architects

4.4.9 **Working with Foam**

Foam has become a very popular material for making quick block models.

The foam is extruded polystyrene, which can be bought from most hardware shops. It is very easy to cut with a utility knife, but ideally you should use a wire cutter.

NB
The wire cutter melts the foam as it is pushed against the wire. This creates toxic fumes, so always use the wire cutter in a well-ventilated area – see **Section 1.3.16**

TIP

Some glues, such as acrylic resin glue, have a chemical reaction with the foam and can 'melt' it. Wood glues can work well with foam.

4.4.10 Working With Card

Take into account the thickness of the card when planning your model. Work to scale for wall thicknesses; you may need to laminate a number of sheets together to achieve the correct dimension. When laminating card, let the glue dry under an even weight to ensure that the card does not buckle. The card pieces will have to overlap in order to achieve a joint, so you should take this into account when cutting your card.

A paper guillotine can be used for cutting paper and card accurately – see **Section 1.3.12**.

NB
Always cut away from your body to avoid accidents.

Take care when cutting very hard materials as the scalpel blade may break – use a utility knife or a fretsaw in the building laboratory.

TIP

Always make a base! This gives the model solidity. You can use a card base, but for larger/more complex models an MDF or plywood base might be more appropriate.

Step 1
Use a piece of scrap card as a 'palette'. Pour out a small amount of glue and use thin cardboard strips to apply the glue to the card.

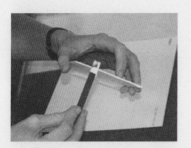

Step 2
Spread the glue evenly along the edge of the card. Avoid using too much glue, as it leaves a mark.

Step 3
Press the card pieces together and use a piece of card to scrape off any excess glue.

4.4.11 Making Curves in Card

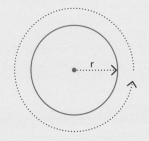

Circumference (c) = 2 × π × radius (r)

π = 3.1416 (to 4 decimal places)

r = 10 mm

62.832 mm = 2 × π × 10 mm

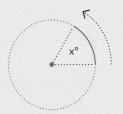

Arc Length (ℓ) = (x° × c) ÷ 360

x° = 60°

10.472 mm = (60° × 62.832 mm) ÷ 360

Step 1
Cut the length of card to the circumference of the circle or length of arc needed *(see formulae above)*. You should allow a little extra card – it is easier to trim the card back later than to try to add a piece.

Step 2

Folding card to achieve a curve will often cause it to crack or split. Scoring shallow parallel lines along the length of the card eliminates this risk. Ensure the lines are evenly spaced and not cut too deeply. Try to maintain the same depth of cut throughout.

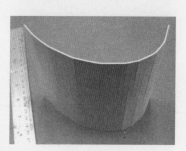

Step 3

Fold the card carefully into the curved shape.

Step 4

If the lines are evenly spaced, you should be able to achieve a neat, even curve to the card.

Secure the card, if necessary, with masking tape as the glue dries.

4.4.12 Making Joints With Card

A **butt joint** is where the two planes of material are glued together with no recess or rebate.

A **recessed** or **rebate joint** works well when you do not want to see the edge of the card – this is useful when using foamboard.

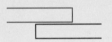

A **chamfered joint** is difficult to achieve in card, but useful in foam models.

A **laminate joint** is when two planes of material are glued together face to face – use this kind of joint to build up thickness of card.

4.4.13 **Making a Recessed Joint**

Step 1

When foamboard is butt-jointed, the edge of the foam remains visible.

Step 2

To get around this, score along the edge of the board to the dimension of the board thickness. Scrape away the unwanted foam section with a scalpel.

Step 3

When the two pieces of foam are glued together, a much neater joint is achieved.

Use sewing pins to pin foamboard pieces before gluing. Do not glue the joints, and use pins to keep part of the model detachable.

4.4.14 Making Cast Models

Cast models are very useful for explaining form, both solid and void. The example here uses Plaster of Paris, but the same principles apply to the casting of other materials, such as wax, concrete and resin.

Wax chippings are available in most craft shops and are melted before being poured into a mould. Extra care must be taken with the joints of the mould, as wax will leak through the smallest of gaps in the card joints.

For concrete casts, cardboard is not strong enough – use plywood or MDF to make the mould. The mould for concrete casts should be screwed and glued together before casting. Line the mould with oil or petroleum jelly to prevent the concrete sticking – this helps you take the mould apart. Any thin oil such as sunflower oil or WD-40 should work.

NB
Concrete casts should be left for at least 24 hours before removing the moulds.

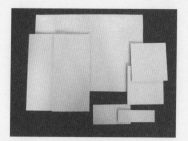

Step 1

Cut out all your card – taking into account that the interior dimensions of your mould will be the final size of the model.

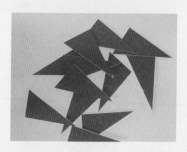

Step 2

Make triangular-shaped cuts of card to use as 'buttresses' on your model. The weight of the wet plaster can distort the card, so these buttresses give the mould extra strength. The buttresses also help maintain square edges.

Step 3

Draw out the position and shape of the mould on a base. This gives you a guide to build your model on. Use a strong piece of card for the base.

Step 4

Build your model on the base. It is common in cast models to make the mould upside down, as this will give you a flat base when the cast is complete. Reinforce any internal changes in form with internal supports.

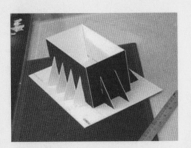

Step 5

Glue the cardboard buttresses around the outside of the mould to give the mould extra strength and rigidity.

Step 6

Use a cloth or your hands to apply petroleum jelly or oil to all internal surfaces – this stops the plaster from sticking. Take extra care to seal the corners as the plaster may leak if there are gaps.

Step 7
Allow the glued mould to dry before mixing the plaster. Spread out newspaper to protect the surface you are working on. Add the Plaster of Paris to a clean plastic container. 1 kg of plaster fills a mould about the size of a standard brick.

Step 8
Add the water slowly, and keep stirring. You need to work fast at this stage as the plaster sets extremely quickly!

Step 9
The plaster should be the consistency of thick porridge. Do not add too much water. If the Plaster of Paris is too runny, it will not set and may leak through any gaps in your mould. If not enough water is added, the plaster sets too quickly and is not workable.

Step 10
Pour the plaster slowly into the mould, making sure it gets into all the corners.

Step 11
Shake the mould to ensure any air bubbles rise to the surface – otherwise these will result in flaws in the final model.

Step 12
Use a flat piece of card to smooth the top surface of the plaster. It is probably easiest to design your mould so that the plaster fills it completely. This allows you to scrape off any excess plaster easily.

Step 13

Leave the plaster to set. The necessary time depends on the amount of plaster used, but setting time should be at least 3 hours.

Make sure to remove the card mould very carefully.

Step 14

You can finish any rough edges of the plaster with a scalpel or sandpaper ...

... and that's it!

5

Surveying

Surveying may be defined as the art of
making measurements of the relative
positions of natural and man-made
features on the Earth's surface, and the
presentation of this information either
graphically or numerically.
—Arthur Bannister, Stanley Raymond,
  Raymond Baker

Surveying existing buildings or sites is a common first step in the design process. Surveying combines careful observation with accurate recording techniques.In this chapter we set out helpful surveying techniques and outline how to compile notes and sketches drawn on site into hard-line drawings. We also outline the ways in which you might observe and draw a site to understand its character. Precise initial survey drawings are critical to the development of accurate and appropriate design proposals. Understanding and analysing any site gives critical information in using the site; we have included here a section on initial site analysis and site planning, using the natural and man-made characteristics of a place to position and plan your proposals.

5.1
Introduction to Surveying

5.1.1 What is Surveying?

There are several methods of surveying, each resulting in varying degrees of accuracy in terms of the information recorded.

The basic tools used in planar surveying are a tape measure for determining distances; a level to determine height or elevation differences; and a theodolite, set on a tripod, to measure long distances and angles, combined with the process of triangulation. Start from a position of known location and elevation. Use an Ordnance Survey (OS) map in the UK and Ireland or the United States Geological Survey (USGS) topographical maps to get this information.

Architects also survey the built environment by drawing and annotating proportional sketches on site.

The purpose of this process is to record information about the proportion, size and relative levels of buildings and elements in plan, section and elevation. This information can then be used to make accurate drawings of existing forms and conditions.

'Surveying' is broadly understood as the objective measurement of a building or site. However, equally important are your analytical and subjective observations. These 'soft' aspects of surveying a site can be critical in developing an understanding of the context of the site and how you might best approach your design. When you initially visit a site take note of your reactions and characteristics such as light, materials, textures and atmosphere.

5.1.2 **Basic Equipment**

Before carrying out any survey, it is a good idea to make a checklist of the equipment you will need to bring with you:

Tape measure

2 mm lead clutch pencil (2B)

3 mm fine pens (black and red)

Eraser

Sketch book

Camera

Clipboard (A4)

Tracing paper

Grid-lined paper

Calculator

Ruler

Compass*

*Most smartphones now have a standard compass app. Other useful apps are available for levels and measuring.

Optional Extras

Laser pointer

Theodolite, dumpy level or spirit level

String

Tape recorder

Mobile phone

TIP

Before visiting a site get a topographical map (from the OS or the USGS). This will provide you with critical information on the site's topography, height and orientation. A laser pointer is a very useful tool if you're surveying on your own. Compass and spirit level apps are available for smartphones.

5.2
Surveying Techniques

5.2.1 Methods of Measurement

Buildings made of modular materials such as brick can be surveyed by measuring the modular brick size and counting the numbers to calculate a length or height.

Most brick buildings in Ireland and the UK are made with bricks that are a standard size of (L) 215 × (W) 102.5 × (H) 65 mm. In the US standard brick dimensions (including mortar) are (L) 8″ × (W) 3 ⅝″ × (H) 2 ¼″. When counting brick courses, always allow 10 mm (⅜″) for a mortar joint between each brick course.

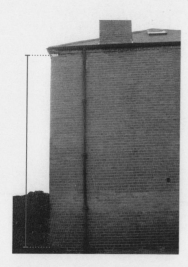

Example 1
79 brick courses from the
ground level to the eaves line.

$79 \times 75^{*}$mm $= 5{,}925$ mm

Overall height $= 5{,}925$ mm

*75mm = 65mm brick height + 10mm mortar joint

In the US, three courses of
brick and mortar = 8".

79 courses ÷ 3 = 26 $\frac{1}{3}$

26 $\frac{1}{3}$ × 8" = 17'-6"

Overall height = 17'-6"

TIP

Before relying on standard brick
sizes, always check the dimensions
of a couple of bricks in case the
bricks are not standard.

Example 2

To calculate the ground slope, measure 10 brick widths along the length of the wall.

Check that the total is 2,250 mm (225 mm × 10). If not, the bricks are either non-standard or have thicker mortar joints than 10 mm.

In Fig. 87, the ground level drops by one brick-height over the length of ten bricks. This is a drop of 75 mm over 2,250 mm. This means 75/2,250 = 1/30 fall.

Brick dimensions vary according to country, but the principle of coordinating brick dimensions remains the same, so check your brick and mortar dimensions before calculating.

Fig. 87

1. Ten-brick-long run
2. Drop of one brick-height

Example 3

Use the same method to calculate other modular elements – for example, the number of window panels on the strip above.

One window panel = 1,010 mm wide

Six window panels in the strip means an overall dimension of (approx.) 6,060 mm wide.

If using I-P measurements, adjust calculations accordingly.

TIP

When calculating multiple elements, always check for thicker outer frame dimensions in case they are different, to ensure an accurate final dimension.

Example 4
Photograph a colleague straight-on against the elevation you want to estimate. To estimate the overall height of the wall, count the approximate number of times your colleague fits into the wall.

Colleague's height = 1.72 m (5'-7⅔")

1.72 × 5.5 = 9.46 m
(5'-7⅔" × 5.5 = 31'-⅓")

Elevation height = 9.5 m (31'-⅓")

NB
Some distortion is inevitable in the photograph due to perspective, so dimensions are approximate only.

Fig. 88

Height and arm span

Fig. 89

Pace

Fig. 90

Hand span

Fig. 91

Foot length

Example 5

Use your body as a measuring device. Know your own dimensions: height, arm span, hand span, foot length and pace.

To calculate your pace (Fig. 89), measure the number of steps you take over a distance of 10 m (30'). Then divide 10 (30) by the number of steps you took to get your pace. This is more accurate than just measuring a single step.

Example 6

To calculate the radius of a column, measure the circumference (Fig. 92) of the column with a piece of string.

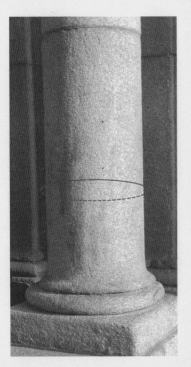

Radius (r) = Circumference (c) ÷ 2π

π = 3.1416 (to 4 decimal places)

c = 1,500 mm

1,500 mm ÷ 2π = 238.73 mm

Fig. 92

Circumference of a column

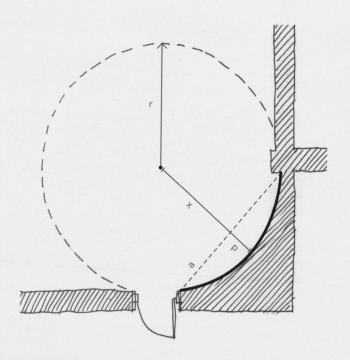

Example 7

To calculate the radius of an arc, first measure the chord length (a) of the arc. Then measure the perpendicular dimension (p) from the mid-point of the chord length to the arc.

The unknown quantity (x) is the distance from the mid-point chord length to the centre of the circle.

Radius $(r) = x + p$

$x = [(a \div 2) \times (a \div 2)] \div p$

if a = 2.4 m and p = 0.65 m

$x = [(2.4 \div 2) \times (2.4 \div 2)] \div 0.65$

then x = 2.215 m

r = 2.215 + 0.65 = 2.865 m

5.2.2 How to Estimate the Height of a Tree

Step 1
Stand directly in front of the tree you want to estimate. Hold a pencil (or any stick) upright in your hand with your arm outstretched in front of you parallel to the ground.

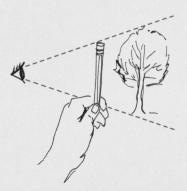

Step 2
Facing the tree, walk backwards until you find the point at which the tree appears to be the same size as the pencil with your arm outstretched. You will need to walk back some distance, so this technique works best where the tree has some open space around it.

Step 3

Turn the pencil 90° in your hand until it appears to lie horizontal on the ground, with the tip of the pencil at the base of the tree.

Step 4

Get someone to stand, at about the same distance from you as the tree, at what appears to be the end point of the pencil (it's easier to do this with one eye closed, but always close the same eye).

Step 5

Measure the distance between the other person and the tree. It's easiest to pace it out if you know your own pace. This gives you the approximate height of the tree.

5.2.3 How to Estimate the Height and Angle of a Hill or Slope

You'll need two people working together.

Person 1 stands at the base of the hill – with a spirit level held horizontally in their outstretched arm (if you don't have a spirit level, use a stick or a spirit level app).

Note the dimension from the ground to Person 1's outstretched arm.

Person 2 walks backwards up the hill until it appears to Person 1 that their feet are at a level with the spirit level.

Person 2 remains in position while Person 1 walks toward them counting out their paces. These two dimensions – Person 1's height and the distance they walk – give you two sides of a triangle. Using Pythagoras' theory, you can work out the slope of the hill.

When Person 1 reaches Person 2's position, the initial steps can be repeated as you move up the hill to get the overall height and angle of the slope.

Person 2   Person 1

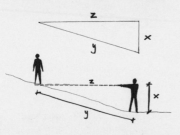

Example

Dimension x = 1.5 m
Dimension y (hypotenuse) = 4.8 m
Dimension z = ?

$x^2 + z^2 = y^2$

$(1.5 \times 1.5) + z^2 = (4.8 \times 4.8)$

$2.25\,m^2 + z^2 = 23.04\,m^2$

$z^2 = 23.04 - 2.25\,m^2$

$z^2 = 20.79\,m^2$

$z = \sqrt{20.79}$

Length of z = 4.55 m

Using trigonometry we can then determine that the angle of the hill is 18°.

5.2.4 OS and USGS Maps

Fig. 93

Before visiting the site, get an Ordnance Survey (OS) or USGS map of the site in question. Digital maps can be obtained from map websites; most have educational versions which your university may have a subscription to. You can use the OS map to check orientation, common routes, levels and topography.

A scale of 1:500 or 1:1,000 is suitable for most small-scale urban studies.

See **https://pubs.usgs.gov/ unnumbered/70039582/report.pdf** for information about USGS Scales.

National Mapping Agency - www.osi.ie

Copyright Permit No. MP 000315

5.2.5 Historic Maps

Fig.94

Detail from John Rocque's Map of Dublin, 1756

When surveying a site, studying historical maps of the area enables you to understand how the site was used previously and how it has developed. Some online map viewers allow you to turn on layers with older maps, which allows you to see sequentially the development of an area. Alternatively, map libraries will hold older printed maps.

Observe street patterns, site and plot lines, and features that remain consistent or have changed. Old maps are also a great source of information on an area's former uses.

5.2.6 On-site Surveying

Sketching onsite results in a deeper, more accurate observation of the site and the buildings on it.

Step 1
When you visit the site, photograph (Fig. 95) and sketch (Fig. 96) it. It can be helpful to mark on a map the locations where the photographs have been taken. 'Straight-on' elevation photos, taken facing the building at a right angle, are a useful reference when drawing up your survey.

Fig. 95

Entrance to the James Joyce Library, University College Dublin, Belfield

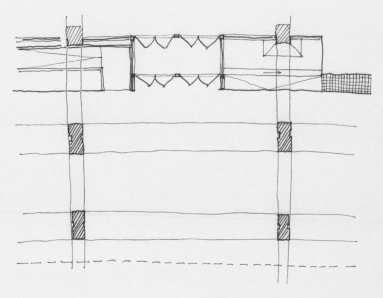

Fig. 96

Sketch plan

Step 2

Draw a sketch plan as accurately as you can, making notes of building elements such as door swings, slopes, ramps and steps. Observe structural elements such as columns and beams lining up, and note what is happening overhead.

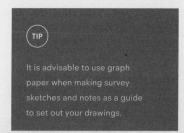

TIP

It is advisable to use graph paper when making survey sketches and notes as a guide to set out your drawings.

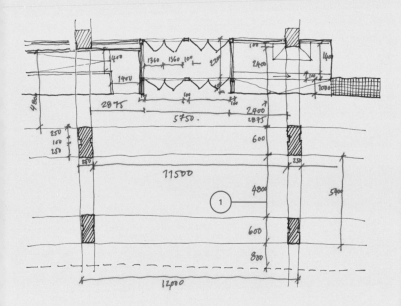

Fig. 97

Plan sketch with annotations

1. Chain dimension

Step 3

Add dimensions to the initial sketch – always try to keep the drawing legible! Take chain dimensions for accuracy. Chain dimensions are a line of continuous dimensions that can be added together to give an overall length.

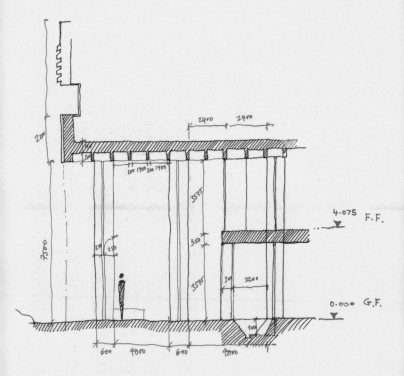

Fig. 98

Section sketch with annotations

Step 4

Now draw a sketch section, taking note of changes in level; alignments; and elements such as overhangs, porches and ceiling details. Once again, take chain dimensions for accuracy.

It is common practice to show finished floor levels in metres.

307

5.2.7 **Surveying an Element**

The following sketches and hard-line drawings are the result of a survey carried out on a window (Fig. 99).

First, draw the object/elevation to be surveyed. This drawing, usually done on an A4 sheet backed by a clipboard and gridded paper, sets up the extent of the object being surveyed. For this reason the setting out of the sheet is key to ensure enough room is left for the object and the related dimensions on the same page.

The sketch (Fig. 100) highlights certain exterior sections of the window to show more detail. Other annotations describe how the window moves.

Fig. 99

Exterior of a Queen Anne window, Marsh's Library, Dublin

Fig. 100 (opposite)

Plan and elevation sketch

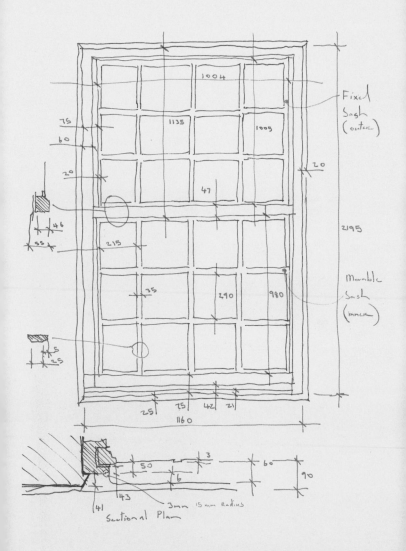

Fixed Sash (outer)

Movable Sash (inner)

Sectional Plan

3mm 15mm Radius

The elevation sketch shown in Fig. 102 gives the general interior layout of the window, plus the seat and timber panelling.

It is similar to the first drawing (Fig. 100), but includes more context. Some further detail is noted at this point also.

Fig. 101
Interior of Queen Anne window,
Marsh's Library, Dublin

Fig. 102 (opposite)
Interior elevation sketch

TIP

Inevitably you will develop your own style of surveying, but clarity and legibility are critical as there may well be a time lapse between when you survey and when you draw up your survey. In an office environment, you may have to draw up a colleague's site sketches or pass on your sketches. While it is advisable to draw up your own survey, if this is not possible legibility is paramount.

Try to avoid making notes without relating them back to the whole object being surveyed.

Taking photographs will help you pull the information together when it comes to drawing up.

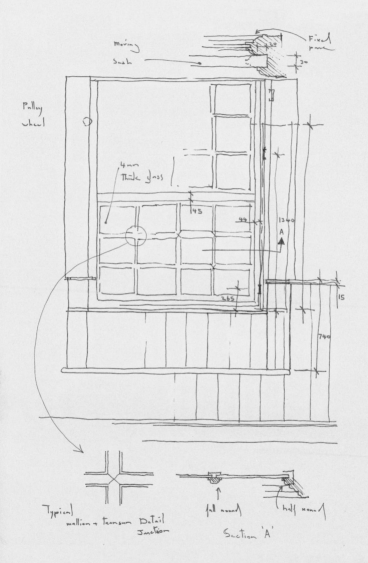

moving
Sash

Fixed
pane

20

30

Pulley
wheel

4mm
Thick glass

45

44

77

1340
A

265

15

740

Typical
mullion + transom DeTail
Junction

full round

half round

Section 'A'

These two sketches are closer studies of window details. They are a more detailed recording of things like the door catch and hinge.

Figs. 103 & 104
Detail sketches

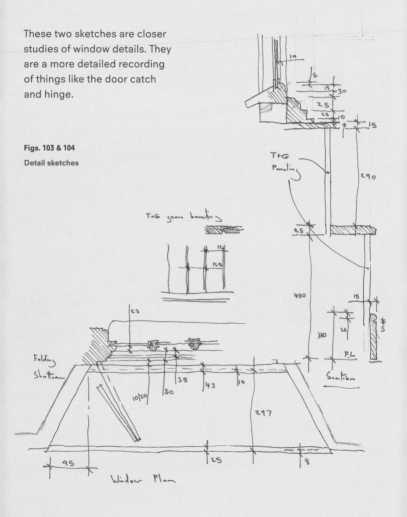

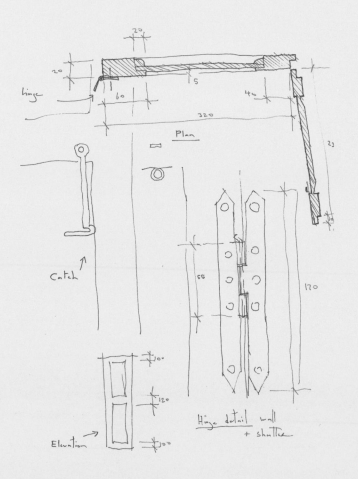

20

20

hinge

60

5

320

40

23

Plan

10

Catch

55

170

100

120

100

Elevation →

Hinge detail wall
+ shutter

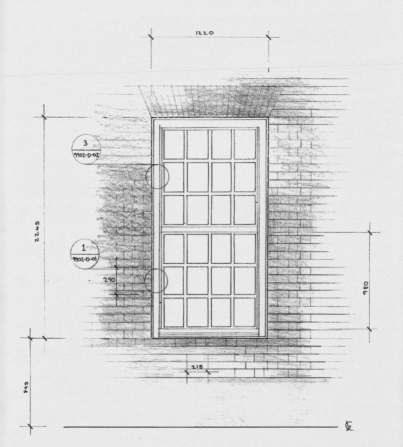

EXTERNAL ELEVATION

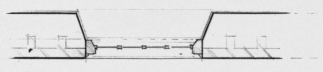

PLAN

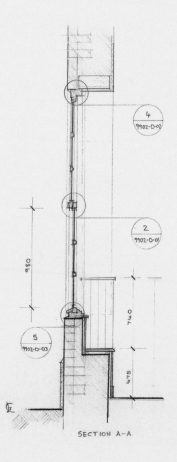

SECTION A-A

The sketch survey information is then used to prepare a hard-line drawing. Laying out the sheet to check that everything fits is important.

These general arrangement elevations and sections can be used to refer to and locate detail drawings.

NB
Always align plan, section and elevation.

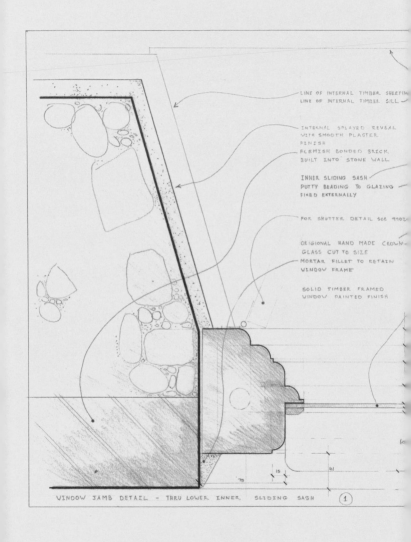

LINE OF INTERNAL TIMBER SHEETING
LINE OF INTERNAL TIMBER SILL

INTERNAL SPLAYED REVEAL
WITH SMOOTH PLASTER
FINISH
FLEMISH BONDED BRICK
BUILT INTO STONE WALL

INNER SLIDING SASH
PUTTY BEADING TO GLAZING
FIXED EXTERNALLY

FOR SHUTTER DETAIL SEE 9902

ORIGINAL HAND MADE CROWN
GLASS CUT TO SIZE
MORTAR FILLET TO RETAIN
WINDOW FRAME

SOLID TIMBER FRAMED
WINDOW PAINTED FINISH

WINDOW JAMB DETAIL — THRU LOWER INNER SLIDING SASH   (1)

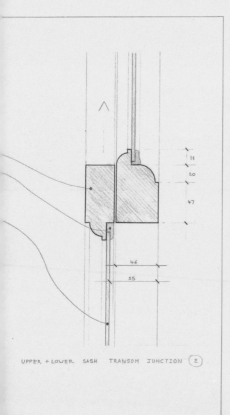

UPPER + LOWER SASH TRANSOM JUNCTION (2)

This 1:2 detail drawing was prepared from the information gathered during the survey, and further research into the history of the window itself.

NB
Some information has been estimated in order to complete the drawing.

3rd Year Architecture	TECHNOLOGY STUDIO	
Project Name:- WINDOW DETAILS - MARSH'S LIBRARY	Project No. 2	
	Date:- 19 - 9 - 10	
Drawing Title:- DETAIL SHEET 1 - Queen Anne Window	Dwg No. 9902 - D - 01	
	Scale: 1:2	

5.3
Material Observation

Case Study: **Beach Promenade**

Developing an intimate knowledge and understanding of materials and how they are used to make buildings is essential for architects.

It is important to build up a knowledge of existing materials, both recent and historic, that have been used in the construction of the buildings, as well as the streetscapes and landscapes, of our cities.

This example shows how you might record the material properties and qualities of an element of architecture while also surveying it. It also highlights the potential when using appropriate materials that relate to context and reinforce an architectural idea.

The promenade design is so subtle – at first you wonder what work has been undertaken in terms of an intervention. But you then become aware of the long linear meandering form the promenade takes.

Beach Promenade, Porto

Architect: Eduardo Souto de Moura.

Project referenced with the kind permission of Eduardo Souto de Moura

You move towards the beach and the view. Leaning on the rail you notice it is warm to the touch, which is unexpected; you may have assumed it would be cold, as its form suggests. It is made of metal, most likely steel. It is painted with some kind of fibrous paint that gives it a textured feel under the hand.

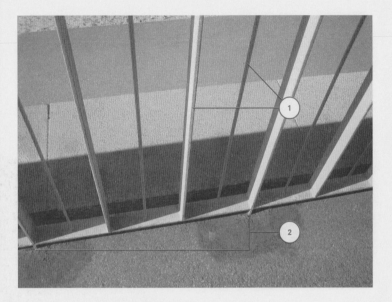

Fig. 105

1. Alternating vertical bar types:
   circular rods and flat metal plates.
2. Railing is fixed to the ground
   every third vertical plate.

The physical experience of
the place draws you into the
design and an understanding
of the project.

On closer inspection you notice
a rhythm and pattern (or order)
to the railing that was not at first
apparent.

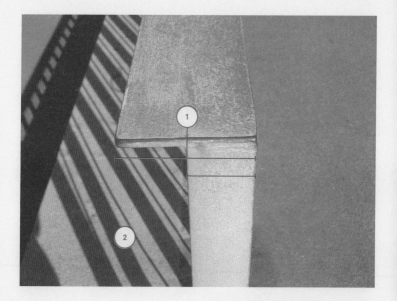

Fig. 106

1. The top rail is twice
   the width of the
   upright section.
2. The shadow creates
   its own pattern.
3. The effect of weathering
   on the metal railing finish
   brings it materially closer
   and in harmony with the
   palette of the beach.

Fig. 107

1. Elements are butt-jointed and welded to each other.

The considered and unobtrusive detailing of the railing, together with its elegant linear form, enhances the design of the promenade and seaside context.

Fig. 108

Sketch elevation

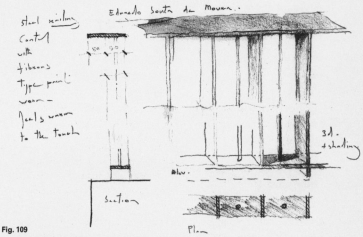

Fig. 109

On-site sketch of railing
form in plan, section and
elevation/3D

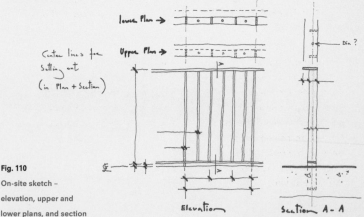

Fig. 110

On-site sketch –
elevation, upper and
lower plans, and section

Case Study: **Student Survey**

Developing an intimate knowledge of materials and how they are used to make buildings and landscapes is an important foundation for architects. It feeds into, and influences, their work at every level of the design process.

The following exercise is an example of a student's responses when asked to study an object/ material on, or close to, their project site by sketching from observation.

Students were specifically asked to:

- Take photographs that record material tone, colour and shadow.
- Sketch this material.
- Record its dimensions, form and proportions in plan, section and elevation.
- Note patterns and observe rhythms.
- Note how it is fixed to the ground/wall.

Example
Gemma Gallagher, 2nd year UCD School of Architecture, 2010/11

Student Description
For my material study, I chose an alleyway leading up to the church beside my site. A lot of the side laneways are very similar, but this one in particular caught my eye as the range of materials used was extraordinary. This lane emphasized the difference between the busy and more modern Martin's Row and the older, traditional narrow streets.

NB
The success of this study lies in the observation of the use of material and relating it to its historical context.

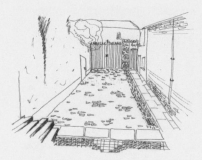

Fig. 111

Overall sketch

Photo of the surfaces

Fig. 112

Photo of the surfaces

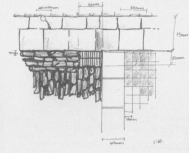

Fig. 113

Photo of the site

Fig. 114

Plan of ground textures

5.4
Site Analysis

5.4.1 Site Analysis Checklist

In addition to surveying, measuring and drawing a site, your initial visits and observations can be critical for making decisions about the scale, placement and form of your projects. Site analysis consists of the objective observation of a site's current characteristics (such as those given in the checklist opposite), but also being aware of the potential of your site as a prompt towards good design strategies.

In the light of our current global climate crisis, using the natural potential of a particular place is vital for reducing the amount of energy needed for heating and lighting, as well as providing more comfortable living environments.

In this section we set out in the following five categories how your site analysis might guide you in making sustainable decisions:

- Orientation
- Shelter
- Sunlight and Solar Gain
- Daylight and Views
- Ventilation

TIP

Photograph the checklist and take it with you on site visits. Annotate a map with the positions of the features listed, because not all of them will be accurately recorded (or visible) on OS or satellite maps.

Site Analysis Checklist

Date and time of visit	
Site orientation	
Access to site	
Access/obstruction to solar radiation	
Prevailing wind/shelter	
Obstacles: access/obstruction to daylight	
Trees (evergreen or deciduous)	
Water courses	
Topography/slope	
Significant level changes	
Water and waste disposal	
Potential renewable energy sources	
Unusual features/aspects	
Significant views	

NB
The on-site checklist is useful
for ensuring you have properly
observed and recorded the
conditions on site.

5.4.2 **Orientation**

The first thing to do when studying a proposed building location is to establish where north, south, east and west are relative to the site. This is what we mean when we refer to orientation in this context. Knowing this allows us to optimize a building's environment by giving access to heat from the sun for:

- space heating
- water heating
- daylight.

The sun's angle relative to the earth's surface varies throughout the year, no matter where in the world we live.

In the northern hemisphere the sun is at its highest at midday on 21st June (summer solstice) and its lowest on 21st December (winter solstice). The reverse is true for the southern hemisphere. However, for the purposes of site analysis we assume the earth is fixed and the sun moves around it.

The diagram opposite demonstrates this with the approximate sun position for a site in Dublin, Ireland:

Winter solstice: 13°
Equinox: 36°
Summer solstice: 60°

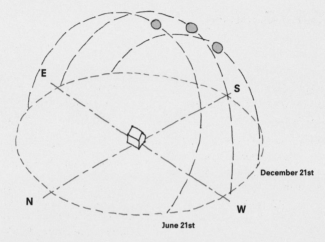

E

S

N

W

December 21st

June 21st

Fig. 115
Sun-path Diagram for Dublin for 12 noon on
21st of December, March and June

TIP

Publicly acessible offical survey
maps, including Google Maps,
are always orientated with north
pointing up. This convention
also applies to plan drawings.

Always include a north
point on your siteplan.

5.4.3 Shelter

Shelter from naturally occurring prevailing winds or unwanted sun can come from:

- the topography (rises and falls) of the site's landscape
- surrounding trees or buildings
- the form of your proposed building design.

A lot can be learned about the local environmental conditions and how they can be harnessed or resolved by looking at how local vernacular buildings are arranged within their site.

Trees and vegetation can act as a sun and wind screen depending on how they are positioned. They also provide privacy. Buildings that sit close to a site can act as wind buffers, but they can also increase the wind levels on your site by virtue of their form and position. In addition to this, surrounding buildings can reduce access to available daylight and sunlight.

The proposed building's form can be positioned in such a way as to create a sheltered outside area that protects against wind yet still allows in sun in the afternoon and evening when it might be most required.

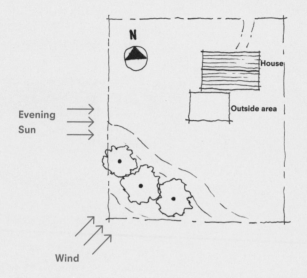

Fig. 116

Plan diagram showing a house sheltered from
southwesterly winds. Note the north point and
external access to evening sun.

5.4.4 Sunlight and Solar Gain

In order to design a building's internal environment it is necessary to understand the external environment and how best to harness the available natural and renewable resources.

As a free resource, the sun is beneficial in several ways:

1. As an infinite, natural and renewable energy source.

2. By allowing occupants to enjoy sun in the internal living environment when it is designed with orientation in mind. This is proven to be important for wellbeing.

3. As a way of creating high-quality, naturally well-daylit interiors.

In cooler climates energy use can be minimized by harnessing the sun's heat for:

- space and water heating via solar panels/air-source heat systems
- thermal-mass heating: an internal floor exposed to sunlight will act as a thermal mass by retaining and radiating heat into the room (this is also known as 'solar gain').

In hotter climates buildings can be kept cool by designing them in such a way that sun is kept out and by including shading devices.

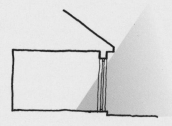

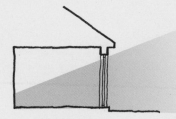

Fig. 117

Diagrams showing the angle of the sun at 12 noon on 21st June (top) and 21st December (bottom) at 53° latitude. Because the hours of daylight at this latitude are shorter in winter, the low angle of the winter sun can penetrate deep into the building.

TIP

It is interesting to know that even a north-facing room will receive some sunlight in the afternoon/ evening for amost half the year at Dublin's latitude of 53° north.

5.4.5 Daylight and Views

Students often confuse daylight and sunlight. 'Daylight' in scientific terms includes both sky light and sunlight. In other words, when the sun isn't shining we still have light from the sky during the day, and it comes equally from all directions – unlike the sun. 'Daylight factor' is the measurement of the percentage of daylight in a room, and is taken assuming an overcast sky.

The relationship between floor-to-window-head height and room depth is an important factor when it comes to daylighting interiors. To create a well-lit space the rule of thumb for single-aspect interiors is a ratio of 1:2 between the window-head height and the room depth (see Fig. 118). For dual-aspect interiors where daylight enters from opposite ends of the room the ratio is 1:4.

At a minimum, the glazed area of the wall in a single-aspect room should be at least 30% of the floor area. The colours of floor, wall and furniture surfaces, and window and room size/shape, will also have a big impact on internal light levels.

The benefit of a northerly aspect (in the northern hemisphere) is that it gives a more constant light, making it most suitable for certain functions like making art.

Provisions for allowing light into a building must be considered alongside the site's potential in terms of views out. The desire to create a thermally efficient building, for example with smaller windows facing north, may conflict with your site analysis and design intentions. A good design will take all site factors into account and balance these with the proposed brief.

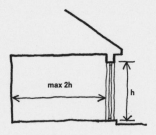

Fig. 118

Rule of thumb for a single-aspect room.

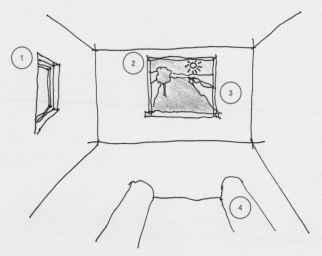

Fig. 119

A well-daylit living space requires:

1. Dual aspect

2. Minimum 2.7m (8'-10") ceiling height/good window-head height and size

3. A view of the foreground, middleground and distance, and of the sky

4. Light-coloured furniture and surface finishes.

5.4.6 Ventilation

Thought should be given to the positioning of rooms of differing functions to best take advantage of the effects of heating and cooling from the external environment. All habitable rooms require fresh air for occupants to breathe, and the air needs to be refreshed throughout the day and night. There are a number of ways to achieve this.

Cross Ventilation: Another benefit of a dual-aspect room is that it allows for a crossflow of air, ventilating the room naturally and passively via vents and window openings. The rate at which the room air will be ventilated will depend on the direction and strength of the wind relative to the room's windows. This is another reason why it helps to know the direction of prevailing winds.

Stack ventilation is another method of passively venting a building. It allows rising hot air to escape at a high level, replacing it with cooler air at a low level. It works best when there is a temperature/pressure difference between inside and outside, when the openings are large enough and there is a significant level difference between the openings.

Heat-recovery ventilation (HRV) is a mechanical system that recycles the heat from hotter rooms in the house (such as bathrooms) and redistributes that heat with fresh air to other rooms in the house. This system allows the air quality and temperature to be controlled and renewed while also saving the energy from this hot air that would otherwise be lost. It works best in airtight buildings and is a common feature in most new-build housing.

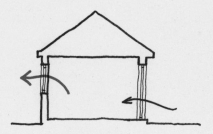

Fig. 120 Cross ventilation.

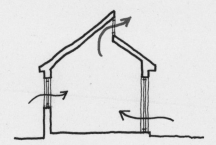

Fig. 121 Stack ventilation.

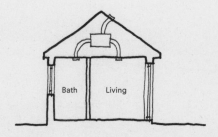

Bath   Living

Fig. 122 Heat-recovery ventilation.

6

Environment & Materials

Again and again there is the sensuality of the material – how it feels, what it looks like: does it look dull; does it shimmer or sparkle? Its smell. Is it hard or soft, flexible, cold or warm, smooth or rough? What colour is it and which structures does it reveal on its surface?
—**Manfred Sack**

The urgency of the climate crisis has resulted in a huge shift in how we design and plan buildings, how we choose materials, and how we future-proof buildings. More fundamentally, we must also question when and why it is necessary to build at all.

Over one third of global carbon output comes from the construction and operation of buildings – architects must be acutely aware of the environmental impact of their decisions. As an architecture student, the climate crisis – and the discipline's response to it – will no doubt shape your education and your career. Radical changes are already occurring to the way architects practice as they address their responsibilities to the future of our planet.

In this chapter we will introduce you to key environmental concepts and terminology as well as describing common building materials. We also set out some issues to do with the selection and use of materials, modular dimensions and the standard sizes of most common construction elements. Environmental considerations are also addressed in Chapter 5 and Chapter 8. This is a reflection of the fact that environmental concerns should be at the forefront of every decision throughout the process of designing a building.

6.1
Environment & Construction

6.1.1 Terminology

Carbon
A common natural element –
C on the periodic table. In terms
of climate change 'carbon' is
sometimes used as shorthand for
carbon dioxide (CO_2), which is the
most significant greenhouse gas
released by human activity. It traps
heat in the atmosphere close to
the surface of the earth.

Greenhouse effect
A naturally occurring process
whereby the atmosphere close
to the earth acts to insulate it.
High levels of CO_2 caused by
human activity have increased
the greenhouse effect, leading to
rising temperatures.

Fossil fuels
Fuels derived from the
decomposition of naturally
occurring organisms. Gas,
petroleum, oil, peat and coal are
all fossil fuels. When burned, these
finite resources release CO_2, which
can increase the greenhouse
effect.

Carbon footprint
The total amount of greenhouse
gas emissions that come from the
production, use and end-of-life of
a human activity. In construction
the carbon footprint is the
measurement of the environmental
impact of a building material,
construction system or building.

Life-cycle analysis
(or life-cycle assessment)
A methodology for assessing
environmental impacts associated
with all stages of the life cycle of
a service, a product or an activity.
It is sometimes called 'cradle to
grave' analysis.

Passive House (or Passiv-haus)
An energy standard for buildings
that are designed to significantly
reduce their heating needs and
energy demand, and so have a
reduced ecological impact. It
concerns the design, construction
and running of buildings.

Retrofit

In construction retrofitting refers to the addition of new technologies or features to older buildings to reduce their environmental impact and minimize energy waste. This would include adding more efficient heating technologies, increasing airtightness and insulation, and replacing single-glazed windows with double- or triple-glazed units.

Adaptive re-use

Refers to the adaption of existing buildings for new purposes – a positive alternative to demolition and re-build.

Operational energy

The energy used in the functioning of buildings, which includes heating, lighting, ventilation and cooling. Retrofitting can significantly reduce the high levels of operational energy used in older buildings.

Embodied energy

The energy used in the extraction, manufacturing and transportation of building materials. Materials with low levels of embodied energy need to be prioritized.

Recycling

Recycling building elements or materials is a positive action that reduces the embodied energy in construction. Some building materials such as metals can be recycled, but the recycled material may be of a lesser quality than its original form. This is known as 'downcycling'.

6.1.2 Reducing the Environmental Impact of Construction

The construction and operation of buildings accounts for approximately 36% of global carbon emissions. With greater awareness of the operational and embodied energy used in construction we also need to be aware of the ecological impacts of waste, water use and biodiversity loss. Architects can act to reduce the environmental impact of construction in the following ways:

1. By prioritizing retrofitting over new building, that is upgrading and insulating existing buildings instead of demolition and new build. Carl Elefante, former president of the American Institute of Architects, said: 'The greenest building is the one that already exists'.

2. By the careful siting and design of buildings to ensure they work with natural light, solar gain, shading and ventilation.

3. By considering the re-use and recycling of building components, and designing and making buildings that are flexible and allow for re-use as building function demands change over time.

4. By looking holistically at the long-term impact of material choices – including how they are made, where they come from and the carbon footprint associated with long-distance shipping, and how they are treated and finished.

5. By designing for reduced levels of energy use within buildings, including minimizing heat loss and maximizing daylighting. As climate change causes rising temperature levels, architects must also design buildings that allow occupants to keep cool during the hottest parts of the year.

For more information on how architects can design and build to higher environmental standards, we recommend *The Environmental Design Pocketbook* by Sofie Pelsmakers, *101 Rules of Thumb For Low Energy Architecture* by Huw Heywood, and *LEED Green Associate Complete Study Guide* by A. Togay Koralturk.

6.2
Introduction to Materials

6.2.1 Wood

Wood (or timber) is easy to work with. It has low weight and thermal conductivity, and high tensile and compressive strength. A variety of grains and hues are available.

Timber is susceptible to decay, but can be treated with natural or chemical applications to add to its longevity. Careful detailing of timber can also help to extend its lifespan.

Timber is an environmentally friendly building product as it is a natural resource and requires low levels of energy in its preparation. Always source timber from an accredited sustainable source.

Common Types
Hardwood: complex cell structure, sourced from deciduous trees.

Softwood: simple cell structure, sourced from coniferous trees.

Uses
Suitable for structural use. Used as a cladding material externally. Also used internally as a lining material and for joinery and furniture.

Environmental Impact
Wood is the most environmentally friendly building product because it has the lowest energy consumption and the lowest CO_2 emissions, it is a renewable resource and is biodegradable. However, the planting of large softwood forests for the construction industry can have a negative impact on habitats and biodiversity. Using locally sourced timber can help reduce the embodied energy of timber. Always source timber from an accredited sustainable source.

Further Reading
Andrea Deplazes, *Constructing Architecture: Materials, processes, structures – a handbook*

Wood Marketing Federation of Ireland, *Woodspec: A guide to designing, detailing and specifying timber in Ireland*

TIP

In the US, building codes distinguish wood elements based on fire resistance. 'Timber' refers to elements larger than 6" × 6", while smaller pieces are called 'lumber' or 'boards'.

6.2.2 Wood Products

These are usually inexpensive composite products made from timber by-products and glue.

They come in a variety of types, and are generally classed according to base wood product and the method of manufacture.

Common Types
Laminates: layers of wood glued together, e.g. plywood and glulam (glued laminated timber).

Particle composite: timber 'chips' bonded together, e.g. oriented strand board (OSB).

Fibreboard: e.g. chipboard, medium-density fibreboard (MDF) and hardboard.

Uses
Most suitable for cladding, formwork and furniture (structural application is possible with glulam products). Some timber products are unsuitable for external use.

Environmental Impact
Timber is a renewable building material, with low levels of embodied energy. However, additional energy is expended in the manufacture of composite timber products, and chemicals are used in the necessary glues and binders. Some engineered wood products use the by-products of timber milling and so reduce waste.

Further Reading
Yvonne Dean, *Materials Technology*, Mitchell's Building Series (see Chapter 13)

TIP

See **Section 6.3** of this chapter for details of the modular dimensions of common wood products.

6.2.3 Stone

Stone is a high-density, high-strength natural material. A wide variety of finishes and textures are available. It belongs to the masonry group of materials.

Key factors in the selection of stone include its hardness, granular size, patterning, colouring and finish. Stone can be finished in a variety of ways – from highly polished to roughly carved, bush-hammered, and so on.

Common Types
Igneous: basalt and granite.

Sedimentary: sandstone, limestone and shale.

Metamorphic: slate and marble.

Uses
Traditionally, stone is used for load-bearing walls and columns. It is now more commonly used as a cladding material. It can be used as a floor surface or for architectural details such as window cills (sills), steps and reveals.

Environmental Impact
As a natural material stone is considered to be reasonably positive in environmental terms. Locally sourced stone should be used where possible to reduce the carbon footprint of long-distance transportation. Large-scale stone quarrying can have negative environmental impacts – including loss of habitats, water pollution caused by chemical runoffs, and the depletion of natural resources.

Further Reading
Joanne Curran, *Stone by Stone – A Guide to Building Stone in the Northern Ireland Environment*

Theodor Hugues, *Dressed Stone: Types of Stone, Details, Examples*

TIP

The key issues to be aware of in stone detailing are:

- the coursing of solid stone walls
- fixings of stone cladding
- the porosity of stone can affect its weathering and staining over time.

6.2.4 Metal

Metal is a high-density material with high thermal and electrical conductivity. There are a wide variety of pure and composite metal alloys available.

Metals are generally finished with a smooth surface, but are prone to corrosion. Alloys are often applied to the surface to reduce this effect.

Common Types
Metals are classified by their chemical composition and density. Heavy metals have a density of 4,500 kg/m³ – e.g. lead, copper, iron and zinc. Light metals are those with a density of less than 4,500 kg/m³ and include aluminium and magnesium. Ferrous metals contain iron, while non-ferrous metals do not.

Uses
Metals such as iron and steel can be used structurally. Sheet metals are commonly used for cladding and roofing. Aluminium window and door profiles are another common use of metal.

Environmental Impact
The extraction of ores (the raw materials used in the production of metals) has a very negative environmental impact – destroying habitats, causing pollution and using high levels of energy. The use of chemicals and energy in the production of finished metal products is likewise damaging to the environment. Where possible specify recycled or recyclable metals such as steel, which does not downcycle.

Further Reading
Burkhard Fröhlich and Sonja Schulenberg, *Metal Architecture: Design and Construction*

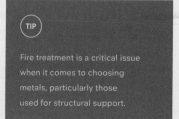

TIP

Fire treatment is a critical issue when it comes to choosing metals, particularly those used for structural support.

6.2.5 Glass

A brittle transparent/translucent material, glass has a high density and compressive strength but it is prone to shattering due to low tensile strength. Its thermal conductivity is average – but this can be improved by applying various coatings and layerings.

Glass is made from metallic oxides and silica which, under very high temperatures, melt to form a liquid. This is cooled to form solid glass.

Common Types
Glass is typically available in sheet form or as blocks. Some types of glass have been developed to deal with specific safety and structural requirements.

Uses
It is most commonly used in windows and doors for light. Structural applications are possible, but expensive.

Environmental Impact
Very large amounts of energy are used in the production of glass, particularly due to the high temperatures needed in the melting of silica – the raw material used in glass production. Glass can be recycled but construction glass often ends up in landfill. Glass is not biodegradable but is inert and doesn't leach harmful chemicals.

Further Reading
Frank Kaltenbach, *Translucent materials: Glass, Plastics, Metals*

Heinz W. Krewinkel, *Glass Buildings: Material, Structure and Detail*

TIP

Be aware of the U-value (see **Chapter 8**) of the glass you choose. Double- and triple-glazing improve the U-value of doors and windows, and help minimize energy wastage.

6.2.6 Brick

Brick is a type of ceramic: an inorganic material with high compressive strength but low tensile strength. It also has low thermal conductivity.

Bricks are made from clay or cement, water and additives, baked at high temperatures to form small modular units. The firing process ensures water resistance.

A wide variety of colours and finishes are available in brick.

Common Types
Clay or cement bricks.

Uses
Traditionally, brick was used for structural applications. Brick is now often used as a cladding or facing material, and can be made in prefabricated panels.

Environmental Impact
High levels of energy are used in the production and firing of clay bricks, and the mining of clay has an environmental impact. Bricks can be salvaged and re-used and have a very long lifespan, mitigating the initial environmental impact of their production.

Further Reading
James W. P. Campbell,
Brick: A World History

Günter Pfeifer et al, *Masonry Construction Manual*

TIP

See **Section 6.3** of this chapter for a description of common brick bonds and for standard dimensions.

Standard brick dimensions can vary according to country of origin.

6.2.7 Concrete

Concrete is a composite material made from cement, water and aggregates. It is fluid initially but sets to form a hard, stone-like material. Admixtures (additives) can be added to concrete to improve elasticity, to speed up or slow down setting times and to add colour.

Concrete is poured into formwork to set, so the design of the formwork combined with the type of aggregate used largely determines the finish of the concrete. Some finishes, such as polishing, are carried out after the concrete has set.

Common Types

Cast in-situ: concrete is poured and set in formwork on site.

Precast: concrete is cast in factory conditions and brought to site as prefabricated solid elements.

Blocks: a common modular form of concrete used in masonry construction.

Uses

Concrete is commonly used for both structural and cladding applications. In combination with steel reinforcement, its structural performance increases.

NB

Cement is a binder: a substance that hardens and can bind other materials together. It is the basic ingredient of concrete and mortar.

Environmental Impact

Concrete has one of the highest environmental impacts of any construction material. Negative impacts include the quarrying of gravel and sand in the production of aggregates, and the high level of energy needed to produce cement. Concrete production results in pollution and, although concrete can be re-used as rubble or landfill, it is not considered a recyclable material. The use of industrial ash by-products in cement can reduce the embodied energy of concrete.

Further Reading

Günter Pfeifer, Antje Liebers and Per Brauneck, *Exposed Concrete: Technology and Design*

David Bennet, *Concrete Elegance*, Volumes 1–4

6.2.8 Insulation

The insulation value of a material is determined by its ability to resist the flow of heat loss from the internal environment.

Insulation can be integrated into the formwork of concrete or inserted as a separate layer in a wall build-up. Insulation has become critical in achieving low-energy buildings.

Common Types
Synthetic: materials such as polystyrene, polyurethane and Rockwool are commonly used.

Non-synthetic: materials such as sheep's wool, straw bales, hemp and cellulose fibres have become increasingly popular due to their environmental benefits.

Uses
Insulation can be applied externally, internally or in a sandwich-style composition in walls, floors and roofs. Insulating materials can be used to form the primary material of construction – such as in straw-bale construction – and also used to insulate against sound transmission.

Environmental Impact
While insulation helps to reduce a building's operating energy use (by reducing heat loss), there are negative environmental impacts in the production of some insulation materials. Fibre insulation materials (cellulose, fibreglass, mineral wool, wood fibre, cotton) have lower environmental impacts associated with their manufacture than foam plastic insulation.

Further Reading
Margit Pfundstein, *Insulating Materials: Principles, Materials, Applications*

6.2.9 Render & Screeds

Typically, cement-based materials are used to cover large areas with few joints.

Render and screeds are generally finish materials that are applied to substrates such as plasterboard or blockwork walls or concrete floors. They are made of a number of materials combined together. In the US external renders are often referred to as 'stucco'.

Common Types

Traditionally, some renders have been made of lime plaster. Recently there has been a rise in the use of synthetic self-coloured renders, which are resistant to fading and shrinking.

Uses

Render and screeds are non-structural and are typically applied to structural elements. Render is commonly used in masonry construction, while screeds are commonly used on concrete floor slabs.

Environmental Impact

The raw-material extraction and quarrying associated with the making of cement- and lime-based renders can destroy natural habitats and landscapes. Cement production has a very high environmental impact, requiring a large amount of energy. Lime-based renders are preferable to cement or synthetic renders as they allow a building to breathe, and can be recycled and removed to allow bricks to be re-used.

Further Reading
Alexander Reichel, Annette Hochberg and Christine Koepke, *Plaster, Render, Paint and Coatings: Details, Products, Case studies*

TIP

Render and screeds shrink when drying, so the inclusion of joints is critical to prevent cracking. Follow the manufacturer's guidelines on the number and placement of movement joints.

6.2.10 Tips When Specifying Materials

1. Where possible use timber in construction; specify timber from sustainably managed sources.

2. Reduce the amount of concrete in your buildings; where possible, specify industrial ash as an aggregate material to reduce the embodied energy of concrete.

3. Choose metals that can be recycled.

4. Use salvaged bricks.

5. Use non-synthetic insulation materials.

6. Use non-toxic finishes and treatments on materials to improve indoor air quality.

7. Use locally sourced materials to reduce the carbon footprint associated with long-distance transportation.

8. Design for the recycling and re-use of building materials and elements; detail for dis-assembly and re-use.

9. Avoid UPVC products for internal finishes and windows – these can compromise indoor air quality and have high embodied-energy levels.

6.2.11 Material Selection Factors

1. **Environmental Considerations**

   Sustainability, source and recycling possibilities are all critical to the selection of materials. This includes the disposal of demolition materials off site and disposal of offcuts and waste during construction. See **Section 6.2.10** for tips on specifying materials to reduce environmental impact.

2. **Structural or Non-structural Application**

   Consider the structural needs of the project when selecting materials (e.g. spans and loads). This will help dictate which materials are appropriate for your particular design.

3. **Cost**

   Consider both the initial cost of the material and the lifetime cost. Some materials may have a low initial cost, but may have a limited lifespan or need regular maintenance. High-cost materials such as natural stone generally have a long lifespan and so may be more cost-effective in the long run.

4. **Location**

   The location of the building project may dictate suitable materials. Sites with high exposure, high levels of pollution or danger of water penetration may rule out vulnerable or high-maintenance materials. Use locally sourced materials where possible, both for environmental reasons and for the aesthetic value of local indigenous materials.

5. Timeframe of Construction	Materials that are labour-intensive, such as bricks traditionally laid, are generally slower than prefabricated materials. With cast in-situ concrete, the curing time needs to be factored into the building programme. If time is a critical issue, prefabricated elements will reduce construction time.
6. Lifespan of the Building	The lifespan of the building needs to be considered when selecting materials. Buildings with a short lifespan, such as a temporary pavilion, may use materials that you would not consider for a permanent structure.
7. Availability	Check the availability of chosen materials before specifying them, as you may have to allow for order and delivery times. This is particularly relevant for materials such as natural stone.
8. Maintenance	Some materials such as external timber cladding require regular maintenance. You should consider this when making your selection, and consult with your client as to the level of maintenance they are willing to undertake. Clients are normally issued with a building maintenance manual, which outlines the maintenance required in a building after completion.
9. Aesthetic Considerations	See **Section 6.2.12** for more detail on the aesthetic considerations of material selection.

6.2.12 Aesthetic Considerations

1. **Weathering**

Weathering of some form occurs with all architectural materials with exposure to rain, wind and sun. Weathering can be *additive* (such as the accumulation of dirt, algae and soot on a material) or *subtractive* (such as the corrosion of stone due to chemical reaction with acid rain).

2. **Jointing**

Two clear strategies emerge in the detailing of joints within materials – either the suppression of joints, to create an impression of mass, or the expression of joints, which leads to a reading of the individual modular elements. Other important considerations are joint colour, thickness and pattern.

3. **Expression**

The choice of materials can impact significantly on the reading of a project. Heavy materials such as cast in-situ concrete give an impression of solidity and permanence. Lightweight materials such as glass and steel give an impression of lightness and transparency.

4. **Fixing**

Fixing methods (particularly for claddings) can be exposed or concealed.

5. **Finish and Treatment**

Most materials allow a range of options for surface finish and treatment. This may serve a purely aesthetic function or, in the case of varnishes and stains on timber, help add to the lifespan of the material.

6. **Colour and Texture**

Colour may be applied through paints or stains – or may be inherent to the material, such as the rich variety of colours available in natural stone.

7. **Morality and Honesty**

This is one of the most complex issues in the aesthetic principles of material selection. Architects and theorists (including Adolf Loos and John Ruskin) have applied morality to the selection of materials, believing that the architect should be 'true' to the material used. 'Honesty' in these terms was understood to mean the exposure of the natural characteristics and colour of the materials, and the avoidance of other materials. Later theorists have questioned the application of morality to building construction.

In this time of climate crisis, morality in terms of selecting building materials may be less to do with aesthetic judgements and more related to choosing materials with the least-negative environmental impact.

6.3
Modular
Materials

6.3.1 Standard Brick Dimensions

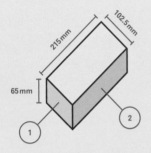

Fig. 123

1. Header (short face of a brick)
2. Stretcher (long face of a brick)

Most bricks in Ireland and the UK conform to standard modular dimensions.

The physical dimensions of a standard brick are:

215 × 102.5 × 65mm*

The coordinating dimensions of a brick are:

225 × 112.5 × 75mm**

Standard US physical dimensions are
7 ⅝ × 3 ⅝ × 2 ¼"

Standard US coordinating dimensions are
8 × 4 × 2 ⅔ "

* Brick manufacturing allows
   for tolerances of ± 2–6mm.
** A 10mm (or ⅜") mortar joint
   allows for this when setting
   out brickwork.

6.3.2 Brick Specials

Special bricks are available from most brick manufacturers and are shaped to allow for easy construction of angles, arches, cills and copings. Brick specials are also commonly used in restoration projects.

The brick specials shown here are available from Kingscourt Country Manor Bricks. For a wider range of brick specials see **www.cmb.ie**, **www.northcotbrick.co.uk** or **www.ibstock.com**

In the US check with manufacturers for dimensions, such as Acme Brick **www.brick.com** or Glen-Gery **www.glengery.com**

NB
Be careful about the colour and texture of brick specials. Always insist on test panels on site, as there can be variations in colour across different brick batches.

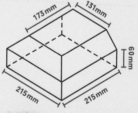

Cant Brick

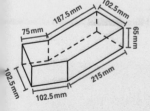

Angled Brick

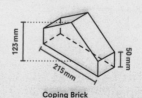

Coping Brick

6.3.3 Standard Concrete Block Dimensions

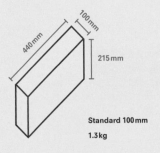

Standard 100 mm

1.3 kg

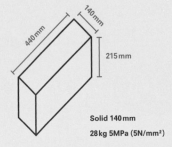

Solid 140 mm

28 kg 5MPa (5N/mm²)

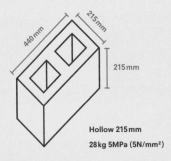

Hollow 215 mm

28 kg 5MPa (5N/mm²)

Concrete blocks come in a range of standard dimensions. The physical dimensions of a standard concrete block are:

440 × 215 × 100 mm

As with bricks, the coordinating dimensions of concrete blocks allow 10mm for a mortar joint:

450 × 225 × 110 mm

In the US the standard concrete block size is 7 ⅝ × 15 ⅝" with thicknesses of 4, 6, 8, 10, 12, 14 and 16". As with bricks, allow ⅜" for mortar joints.

6.3.4 Concrete Block Variations

The page opposite shows three common block sizes. However, there are a number of variations that may be used for specific purposes, such as cavity closers or lintels, or for appearance or strength – e.g. soap bar blocks.

Blocks also come in a variety of finishes and strength classes. Exposed or 'fair-faced' blockwork is commonly constructed using a finer-grade aggregate for a smoother finish.

See **www.roadstone.ie** or **www. thomasarmstrongconcreteblocks. co.uk** for more details on concrete blocks. For block variations in the US, see the National Concrete Masonry Association website **www.ncma.org**

450 Range
Coordinating face size (including mortar joints) of 450 × 225 mm giving 9.88 blocks per m²

In the US the coordinating face size of 8" high and 16" long would require two blocks per ft²

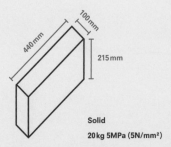

440 mm
100 mm
215 mm

Solid
20 kg 5MPa (5N/mm²)

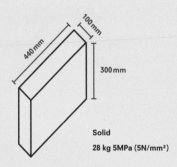

100 mm
440 mm
300 mm

Solid

28 kg 5MPa (5N/mm²)

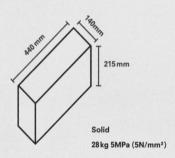

140mm
440 mm
215 mm

Solid

28 kg 5MPa (5N/mm²)

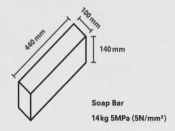

100 mm
440 mm
140 mm

Soap Bar

14 kg 5MPa (5N/mm²)

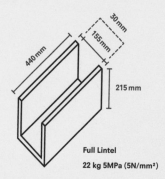

Full Lintel

22 kg 5MPa (5N/mm²)

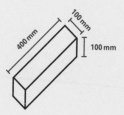

Soap Bar

10 kg 5MPa (5N/mm²)

Filler Block

3 kg 15MPa (15N/mm²)

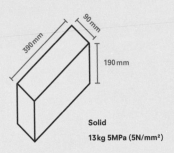

Solid

13 kg 5MPa (5N/mm²)

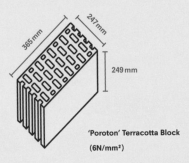

'Poroton' Terracotta Block

(6N/mm²)

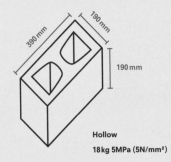

Hollow

18 kg 5MPa (5N/mm²)

6.3.5 **Brick & Block Modules**

Bricks and concrete blocks work in modules – this allows for ease of construction of combined block- and brickwork. The illustration below shows how bricks and blocks work together. This means courses can be aligned to allow ease of setting out for openings and for the insertion of elements such as wall ties.

In the US, one block 7 ⅝" tall + ⅜" mortar joint on the bottom grids out at 8" and aligns with three courses of brick (three bricks plus three mortar joints). One block 15 ⅝" long + ⅜" mortar joint grids out at a 16" module and aligns with two stretchers of modular brick (two bricks plus two mortar joints).

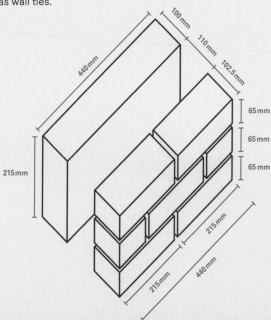

6.3.6 Brick Bonds

Stretcher Bond

This is the most commonly used modern brick bond because it is the simplest to construct for single-leaf brickwork walls or for brick cladding. Known as a running bond in the US.

This bond is less common in historical brick buildings.

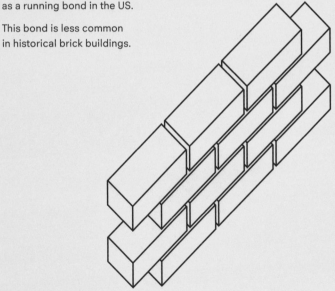

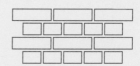

English Bond

This bond was often used for solid brick walls as the combination of stretchers and headers allowed for easy construction of solid double-brick-thick walls.

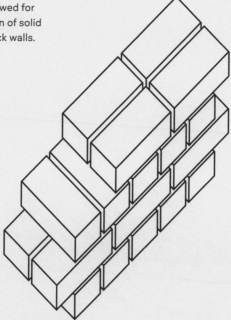

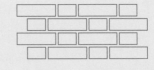

Flemish Bond

An even, regular rhythm of stretcher, header, stretcher.

Also commonly used in solid brick walls, and therefore less common in modern construction.

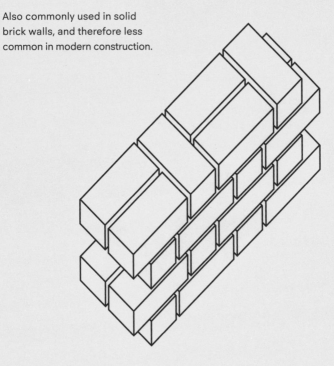

Stack Bond or Unbonded
The regular grid means this
type of brick bond is not
suitable for structural uses
and is typically used for infill
or cladding purposes.

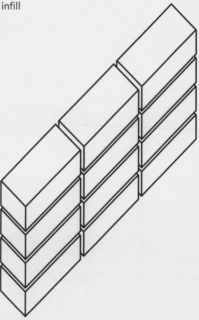

Stack Bond or Unbonded
Again, the regular grid means this type of brick bond is not suitable for structural uses and is typically used for infill or cladding purposes.

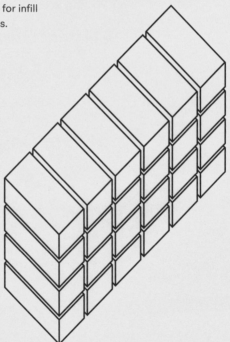

Soldier Course

Usually found over a window or opening, forming the window or door head. Can be threaded through with reinforcement bars or supported by a steel lintel.

A soldier course is sometimes integrated into a solid wall for decorative effect.

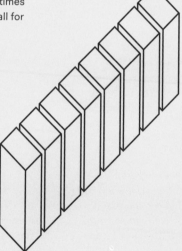

6.3.7 Sheet Material

	Height	Width	Thickness
Plywood	2,440 mm (8')	1,220 mm (4')	4; 6.5; 9; 12; 15; 18 mm (variety) *
OSB	2,440 mm (8')	1,220 (4')	9; 11; 18 mm (variety) *
MDF	2,440 mm (8')	1,220 (4')	3.5; 6; 9; 12; 15; 18; 25; 32 mm (variety)
Hardboard	2,440 mm (8')	1,220 (4')	3.5 mm (⅛")
Chipboard	2,440 mm (8')	1,220 (4')	15; 18 mm (½; ¾") *
Acrylic	2,050 mm (6'-8")	1,016 (3'-4")	3; 4; 5; 6mm (variety) *

*Other sizes available

Oriented Strand Board (OSB)

OSB is an engineered wood product formed by layering strands of wood chips in specific orientations. These are compressed and bonded together with wax and resin.

MDF

This is also an engineered wood product made from fine wood fibres that are heated under pressure and combined with wax and resin. MDF is more dense than plywood.

Most timber sheet material sizes have their origins in imperial dimensions (feet and inches).

There is a good selection of sheet material available from Strahan Timber. Their website is also a good source of information on finishes and sizes of timber-based sheet material (see **www.strahan. ie**). Information can also be found at **www.mstc.co.uk**. In the US information can be found at **www.apawood.org**

6.3.8 Sheet Glass

	Max. Height	Max. Width	Thickness
Clear Float	3,000mm (9'-10")	1,600 (5'-3")	2–19mm
Toughened	4,500mm (14'-9")	2,500 (8'-2")	6mm
	2,720mm (8'-11")	1,270 (4'-2")	4–19mm
	2,550 (8'-4")	1,550 (5'-1")	4–19mm
Laminated	2,440 (8')	1,220 (4')	4.4–45mm

Toughened Glass
Toughened (or tempered) glass has increased strength compared with standard sheet glass. The benefit of toughened glass is that it will, if broken, shatter into small pieces. As such, it is less likely to cause injury.

Laminated Glass
Laminated glass has a middle layer of polyvinyl between two or more layers of glass. This layer prevents the glass from breaking up into large pieces when the glass is smashed, as the sheet remains in one piece.

In the US thickness is normally measured in metric rather than I-P.

More information on glass dimensions can be found in the *Architect's Pocket Book* by Charlotte Baden-Powell (p. 269).

General information can be found at **www.pilkington.com** and **agcglass.com**

6.3.9 Glass Blocks

Length (mm)	Width (mm)	Depth (mm)
115	115	80
190	190	80 *or* 100
240	240	80
240	115	80
300	300	100

Typically there is a 10mm (⅜ ") mortar joint between glass blocks.

U Glass

This product is a cast glass with a U-shaped profile that is translucent but not transparent. It has good strength and insulation properties.

In the US standard dimensions are 8 × 8 × 3".

For a full range of U Glass information, see **http://uglass.net**.

6.3.10 Other Materials

Slate

A good range of slate products, dimensions and finishes are available from the following suppliers:

www.bluebangor.ie

www.sigroofing.ie

www.marleyeternit.co.uk

www.redland.co.uk

www.tegral.com

www.americanslate.com

Fibre Cement Panels

A range of fibre cement panels are available from:

www.tegral.com

www.americanfibercement.com

6.3.11 Softwood Timber Sizes

Standard Sawn Softwood Timber Sizes (12–44 mm)

(mm)	25	38	50	75	100	125	150	175	200	225	250	300
12	•	•	•	•	•		•					
16			•	•	•	•	•					
19	•	•	•	•	•	•	•	•				
22				•	•	•	•					
25	•	•	•	•	•	•	•	•	•	•	•	•
32				•	•	•	•	•	•	•		•
36				•	•	•	•					
38			•	•	•	•	•	•	•	•		•
44				•	•	•	•	•	•	•	•	•

These charts (above and opposite) refer to sawn timber sizes (i.e. the timber is still relatively rough). Finished timber is planed and the dimensions shown are reduced.

NB
Rough sawn timber is slightly larger than finished timber. This allows for the shrinkage associated with planing and drying (in the US dressing or surfacing).

Softwood
Softwood refers to wood from coniferous trees, such as fir, pine and spruce. In general it is relatively easy to work and is used widely in the construction of buildings. There is a difference in terminology between US and European construction. In the US 'timber' refers only to wood elements larger than 6 × 6 ″. 'Lumber' refers to smaller wood elements.

Standard Sawn Softwood Timber Sizes (47–300 mm)

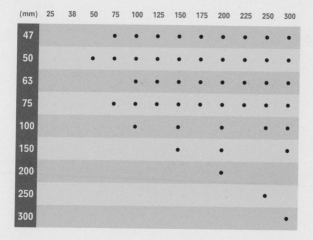

(mm)	25	38	50	75	100	125	150	175	200	225	250	300
47				•	•	•	•	•	•	•	•	•
50		•	•	•	•	•	•		•		•	•
63				•	•	•	•	•	•		•	•
75			•	•	•	•	•	•	•		•	•
100				•			•		•		•	•
150						•			•			•
200									•			
250											•	
300												•

Reduction from sawn sizes by planing:

Structural Timber
3 mm up to 100 mm
5 mm over 100 mm

Joinery/Cabinetry
7 mm up to 35 mm
9 mm over 35 mm
11 mm up to 150 mm
13 mm over 150 mm

In the US the reduction from nominal to actual size is ¼" up to 2" (boards), ½" up to 5" (dimension lumber), ¾" off 7" to 16" and then finally 1" off anything bigger than 16".

A 1 × 4 measures ¾" × 3 ½"
A 2 × 6 measures 1 ½" × 5 ½"
A 3 × 6 measures 2 ½" × 5 ½"
A 6 × 6 measures 5 ½" × 5 ½"

See table American Softwood Lumber Standard PS-20: http://www.alsc.org/untreated_ps20_mod.htm

6.3.12 Hardwood Timber Sizes

Standard Sawn Hardwood Timber Sizes (19–100 mm)

(mm)	50	63	75	100	125	150	175	200	225	250	300
19			•	•	•	•	•				
25	•	•	•	•	•	•	•	•	•	•	•
32			•	•	•	•	•	•	•	•	•
38			•	•	•	•	•	•	•	•	•
50			•	•	•	•	•	•	•	•	•
63					•	•	•	•		•	
75					•	•	•	•	•	•	•
100				•	•	•	•	•	•	•	

This chart refers to sawn timber sizes. Finished timber is planed and the dimensions shown are reduced.

Planing is the process used to give a smooth surface to a rough piece of timber. (In the US hardwood is less standardized – check with your supplier.)

Reductions from sawn sizes by planing are as follows:

Structural Timber
3mm up to 100 mm
5mm for 101–150 mm
6mm for 151–300 mm

Wood Trim
6mm up to 25 mm
7mm for 26–50 mm
8mm for 51–100 mm
9mm for 101–105 mm
10mm for 151–300 mm

Joinery/Cabinetry
7mm up to 25 mm
9mm for 26–50 mm
10mm for 51–100 mm
12mm for 101–150 mm
14mm for 151–300 mm

Flooring
5mm up to 25 mm
6mm for 26–50 mm
7mm for 51–300 mm

6.3.13 Glulam Beam Sizes

Common Glulam Beam Sizes (180–1,035 mm)

(mm)	65	90	115	140	165
180	•				
225	•	•			
270	•	•			
315	•	•			
360		•	•	•	
405		•	•	•	
450		•	•	•	
495			•	•	•
540			•	•	•
585				•	•

(mm)	115	140	165	190	215
630		•	•		
675		•	•	•	
720			•	•	
765			•	•	•
810				•	•
855				•	•
900				•	•
945				•	•
990					•
1,035					•

Glulam is a type of structural timber composed of several layers of timber glued together. This laminating process enables greater spans using timber, which has a lower embodied energy than steel or concrete. Glulam beams and columns can be ordered to specific sizes; check with your local manufacturer.

For further information on glulam dimensioning, loads and specification, see **www.glulambeams.co.uk** and in the US **www.apawood.org/glulam**

6.3.14 Standard Steel Sections

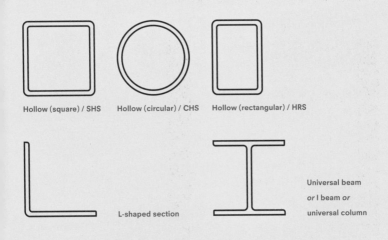

Hollow (square) / SHS   Hollow (circular) / CHS   Hollow (rectangular) / HRS

L-shaped section

Universal beam
or I beam or
universal column

Hot-rolled Steel
This is steel formed by heating and rolling. There is greater dimensional variation when compared with cold-rolled steel.

Cold-rolled Steel
In this process, steel is formed at room temperature. This gives a better finish and allows tighter tolerances.

NB
The internal radius of any right-angled steel section will be equal to, or greater than, the thickness of the steel.

6.3.15 Hot-rolled Steel Sizes

Square	Circular*	Rectangular	Universal**
40 × 40 mm	26.90 mm	50 × 30 mm	406 × 140 mm
50 × 50 mm	42.40 mm	60 × 40 mm	356 × 171 mm
60 × 60 mm	48.30 mm	80 × 40 mm	356 × 127 mm
70 × 70 mm	60.30 mm	90 × 50 mm	305 × 165 mm
80 × 80 mm	76.10 mm	100 × 50 mm	305 × 127 mm
90 × 90 mm	88.90 mm	100 × 60 mm	305 × 102 mm
100 × 100 mm	114.30 mm	120 × 60 mm	254 × 146 mm
120 × 120 mm	139.70 mm	120 × 80 mm	254 × 102 mm
140 × 140 mm	168.30 mm	150 × 100 mm	203 × 133 mm
150 × 150 mm	193.70 mm	160 × 80 mm	203 × 102 mm
160 × 160 mm	219.10 mm	200 × 100 mm	178 × 102 mm
180 × 180 mm	244.50 mm	200 × 120 mm	152 × 89 mm
200 × 200 mm	273.00 mm	200 × 150 mm	127 × 76 mm
250 × 250 mm	323.90 mm	250 × 100 mm	
300 × 300 mm	406.40 mm	250 × 150 mm	
350 × 350 mm	457.00 mm	300 × 100 mm	** These are nominal sizes.
400 × 400 mm	508.00 mm	300 × 200 mm	Allowances should be
		400 × 200 mm	made for tolerances.
		450 × 250 mm	
	* Diameter sizes	500 × 300 mm	

For further information on steel
in the US, see the American
Institute of Steel Construction
Steel Manual or website:
www.aisc.org

6.3.16 Cold-rolled Steel Sizes

Square	Circular*	Rectangular	Universal**
25 × 25 mm	26.90 mm	50 × 25 mm	406 × 140 mm
30 × 30 mm	33.70 mm	50 × 30 mm	356 × 171 mm
30 × 40 mm	42.40 mm	60 × 30 mm	356 × 127 mm
50 × 50 mm	48.30 mm	60 × 40 mm	305 × 165 mm
60 × 60 mm	60.30 mm	70 × 40 mm	305 × 127 mm
70 × 70 mm	76.10 mm	70 × 50 mm	305 × 102 mm
80 × 80 mm	88.90 mm	80 × 40 mm	254 × 146 mm
90 × 90 mm	114.30 mm	80 × 60 mm	254 × 102 mm
100 × 100 mm	139.70 mm	90 × 50 mm	203 × 133 mm
120 × 120 mm	168.30 mm	100 × 40 mm	203 × 102 mm
140 × 140 mm	193.70 mm	100 × 50 mm	178 × 102 mm
150 × 150 mm	219.10 mm	100 × 80 mm	152 × 89 mm
160 × 160 mm	244.50 mm	120 × 40 mm	127 × 76 mm
180 × 180 mm	273.00 mm	120 × 60 mm	
200 × 200 mm	323.90 mm	120 × 80 mm	
250 × 250 mm	355.60 mm	140 × 80 mm	** These are nominal sizes.
300 × 300 mm	406.40 mm	150 × 100 mm	Allowances should be
	457.00 mm	160 × 80 mm	made for tolerances.
	508.00 mm	180 × 80 mm	
		180 × 100 mm	
		200 × 100 mm	
	* Diameter sizes	200 × 120 mm	
		200 × 150 mm	
		250 × 150 mm	
		300 × 100 mm	
		300 × 200 mm	
		400 × 200 mm	

Advantages of Cold-rolled Steel

- It has greater strength than hot-rolled steel for the same size section.

- Very tight tolerances are possible, and can be consistently repeated when more are required.

- A great range of shapes is possible.

- A high-quality finish is possible.

- Conventional jointing methods (such as riveting, bolting, welding and adhesives) can be used.

- Cold-rolled steel tends to be lighter, making it easy to transport and erect.

In the US, for elements that are cold-formed and up to about one inch thick, see the American Iron and Steel Institute website: **www.steel.org**. For larger structural members (even if cold- rather than hot-rolled) see **www.aisc.org**

7

Structure

Engineering as a catalyst to inspire creativity is not the generally held view. But in the Greek word *techne*, the unity of engineer–architect describes a sharing of design values, the diagram and calculation, the concept and proportion being viewed as cycles of poetic invention.

The mystery is in the unseen calculation of exact balance, of up versus down, of substance versus immateriality, of light against shadow.
—Cecil Balmond

Structures are designed for strength, stability and durability. The fundamental purpose of any structure is to transmit loads from the point of application to the point of support, and ultimately through the foundations to the ground. The design process requires an architect to have a good knowledge and understanding of the nature of structure and the various elements involved, so that they can best exploit its potential. A structural engineer will typically analyse and design the structure in detail to ensure adequate performance.

During your architectural education you will probably take classes in structures (or statics), mechanics and building physics. In this chapter we set out the key terminology and concepts of structures, explaining some basic structural forms and conditions. We then go through the sizing of structural elements and give some rules of thumb for the use of timber, concrete and steel elements in the early design stages. Finally, we show one case study that highlights the potential structure has as an integrated element in a design.

7.1
Structural Principles & Terminology

The structure of a building comprises the load-carrying elements that enable the building to stand up and withstand loads and movement. To achieve a successful structural design, engineers and architects should use materials efficiently for economy and elegance. An appreciation of how forces act on a building and the characteristics that govern how materials behave structurally will allow you to understand the structural systems that you'll use in your own designs.

7.1.1 Forces

A force is a push or a pull on an object which can result in that object moving or changing shape. There are five common forces:

Tension is a pull force, like a tug of war where the rope is in tension as forces are applied at either end, pulling it taut.

Compression is a push force. When you sit on a chair you are applying compression through the weight of your body on the seat.

Moment is a bending force, which varies depending on the load being applied and the distance the force is from the support. Think of walking to the end of a diving board – the diving board bends more as the load (your weight) travels further from the support. Moment is calculated by multiplying the force by the distance (from the support).

Torsion is a twisting force applied to one end of an object while the other end is fixed (or is being twisted in the opposite direction). When you wring water from a wet towel you are applying torsional force to the towel.

Shear is a force created by two adjacent pushing or pulling forces acting perpendicular to the structural element, resulting in a 'tearing' action, like scissors cutting through paper.

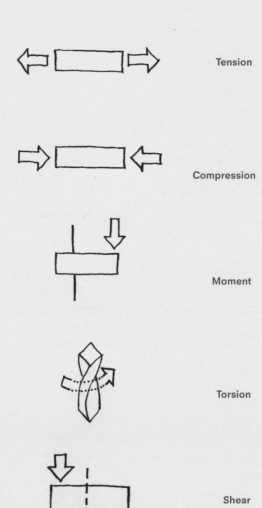

Tension

Compression

Moment

Torsion

Shear

7.1.2 Loads

Force is measure of the interaction between two bodies. In metric, 1 Newton (N) of force is defined as the amount of force needed to accelerate 1 kilogram (kg) of mass at a rate of 1 metre per second squared (m/s^2). Its unit is kg m/sec^2. In I-P, force is measured in pounds (lb) or kilopounds (kip), where 1,000 lb = 1 kip.

Load is a force acting on a structural element. In metric loads are measured in kN/m^2. In I-P they are measured in pounds per square foot, or psf (lb/ft^2). Building loads can be divided into three broad categories:

Dead load is the weight of the structure itself, including any permanently fixed items.

Live load is a moving or variable load added to the building (e.g. occupants or loose furniture) and the loads caused by wind, snow and rain.

Imposed load is any load which the structure must sustain other than the weight of the structure itself, but excluding wind load (these could be impact loads or earthquakes).

Structural engineers will calculate the total anticipated loads on a building in order to design the most efficient structure to carry these loads.

Fig. 124

Building loads:

1. Dead load: the load of the fabric of the building.

2. Live load: including building occupants and furniture, wind, rain and snow.

3. Imposed load: including impact and vibration.

7.1.3 Material Characteristics

Common construction materials (timber, glass, concrete) behave differently under the application of forces. We can describe the characteristics of building materials under the following terms:

Strength is the measure of a material's ability to resist deformation under the application of loads. If a material resists pulling forces well it is high in tensile strength. If it resists compression forces it is high in compressive strength.

Stiffness is a material's ability to resist bending. Stiff materials do not deflect or bend easily under the application of forces.

Elasticity is a material's ability to regain its original shape after external pressure has been removed, like an elastic band.

Plasticity is a material's ability to retain its deformed shape after external pressure has been removed. Rolled-out dough retains its 'new' shape after the force of the rolling pin has been removed.

Brittleness is a property in which material breaks with little deformation when subjected to stress. When glass breaks it does not deform (or bend) significantly before breaking.

7.1.4 Definitions of Common Terms

Span is the horizontal distance between supports for a structural element.

One-way span describes a horizontal structural element that spans in one direction, for example between two parallel walls.

Two-way span describes a horizontal structural element that spans in two directions, for example a floor slab supported by four walls or columns.

Bending moment is the deformation inducted in a structural element on the application of external forces.

Equilibrium is the state in which all the forces acting upon an object are balanced.

Cantilever is a rigid structural element supported at one end only, for example a diving board or projecting balcony.

One-way span

Two-way span

Bending moment

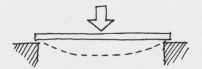

Equilibrium

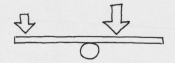

Cantilever

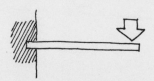

Stress is a physical quantity that defines the force per unit area applied to a material. There is lower stress when the force is spread over a larger area, and higher stress when the same load is applied over a smaller area.

Bracing or cross-bracing are structural elements used to withstand buckling of a structure under external loads. Bracing maximizes the loads a structure can support.

Structural unit describes a structural bay that is often repeated to compose a building.

Structural grid is the underlying order or pattern applied to the positioning of structural elements.

Isotropic describes the characteristic whereby a material behaves the same in all directions. Steel is an isotropic material.

Anisotropic is the characteristic whereby a material behaves differently in each direction. Timber behaves differently according to whether loads are applied parallel or perpendicular to the grain of the wood.

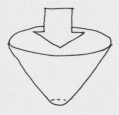

High stress – load supported by a small surface area

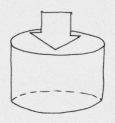

Low stress – load supported by a large surface area

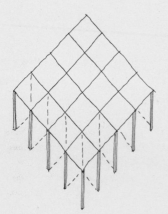

A composition of structural units

Structural grid

7.2
Structural Systems

A structural system consists of the elements of a building that act structurally, bringing the building loads to the ground. In your own designs, it is important to plan the most appropriate underlying structural order: what is supporting the floors and roofs and what is carrying the building loads to the ground. Some structural systems, such as columns and beams, allow more flexible spatial planning, whereas load-bearing walls result in cellular, room-type structures. It is therefore useful from a design perspective to have an understanding of the limits and possibilities of the various construction materials in terms of their structural use.

In multi-storey buildings, it is most efficient to transfer vertical loads from one load-bearing element directly to the next. This means lining up vertical structural elements – walls or columns – on multiple floor plates. For this reason, the size of the structural grid and the location of your load-bearing elements is one of the most significant design decisions.

7.2.1 Classifying Structural Elements

There are various ways to categorize structural systems: by the type of material used, by the length of spans achievable or by how they carry/transfer loads. Here we have classified common structures in terms of their primary means of transferring loads (horizontal or vertical), and have included a section for three-dimensional structures.

In this section we describe common structural elements in three categories:

Vertical Elements
Walls
Columns
Foundations
Retaining walls

Horizontal elements
Beams
Slabs
Arches
Vaults
Folded Plates
Trusses
Girders

Framed, Shell and Tensile Structures

This guide is a basic overview – for more details on how these structures work, we recommend *Introduction to Architectural Technology*, by Silver and McLean, and *Tony Hunt's Sketchbook*.

7.2.2 Vertical Structural Elements

The primary structural function of vertical elements in a building is to transmit loads from the building roofs and floors to the foundations.

There are numerous types of wall and column that can perform this function.

1 Walls Structural or load-bearing walls can be solid (such as masonry or cast in-situ concrete) or frame walls (such as timber). For more information on the construction of walls **see Chapter 8 – Principles of Construction**.

2 Walls with piers Light or thin structural walls can be strengthened by the presence of piers or buttresses.

3 Columns Columns carry loads vertically, eliminating the need for load-bearing walls and thus freeing up the plan. Structural columns are typically made of steel, concrete (usually reinforced with steel) or timber.

4 Retaining walls – see **Section 7.2.4**.

5 Foundations – see **Section 7.2.3**.

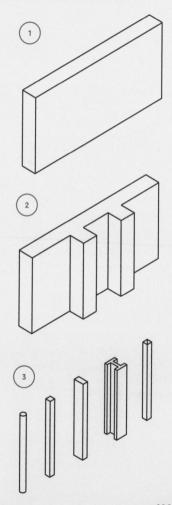

7.2.3 Foundation Types

All structures require a foundation to take all the loads safely to the ground. This is to avoid uneven settlement or, in the worst case, structural failure.

The choice of foundation design is influenced primarily by three factors:

1 The size, weight and contents of the building – its total load.

2 The type of soil/rock the building will sit on. This is determined by soil investigations at an early design stage, and informs the engineer of the load-bearing capacity of the soil.

3 The structural system used: for example, for a building using columns as the vertical structural elements, pad foundations are most suitable.

NB

As soil under the building compresses, the building sinks slightly. This is called settlement.

Load-bearing capacity (LBC) refers to a soil's ability to support loads without undue distortion.

Strip Foundation

A strip foundation provides a continuous support to a load-bearing wall below ground.

It is commonly used for domestic-scale construction, and contains steel to reinforce the concrete when under tension.

Concrete as a material performs well under compression but not when tension is applied.

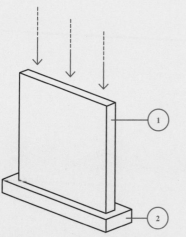

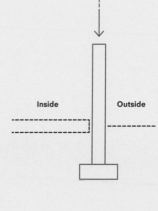

Fig. 125

1. Wall

2. Strip foundation with steel reinforcement

Raft Foundation

A raft foundation is used where the load-bearing capacity of the soil is not good, but it can bear a continuous slab where the loading is spread out over the whole slab.

The edges of the slab are deepened to take the load of the walls. A raft foundation is thicker than a ground-bearing slab and 'floats' on the ground.

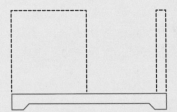

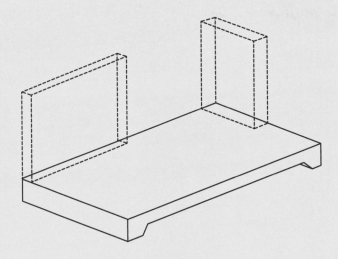

Pad Foundation

A pad foundation is used where the support required is at specific points where the structure meets the ground.

A 'framed' structure, where the load is carried to the ground through columns, is an example of where pad foundations would be used.

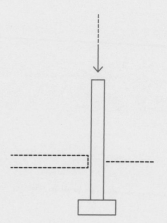

Pile Foundation

A pile is a cylindrical-shaped form either driven into or cast in the ground to support a structure above ground.

A pile foundation is used when a solid footing, such as bedrock, is a long distance below the ground-floor level. In this case, a precast pile is driven into the ground under force or a pile hole is made and filled with reinforcing steel and concrete.

Piles can be either grouped together and connected with a pile 'cap', or they can be joined by a ground beam.

Piles are classified as deep foundations, and are most commonly used in medium- to high-rise construction.

Fig. 126

1. Ground beam
2. Structure above ground/column
3. Pile cap
4. Pile
5. Contiguous piles

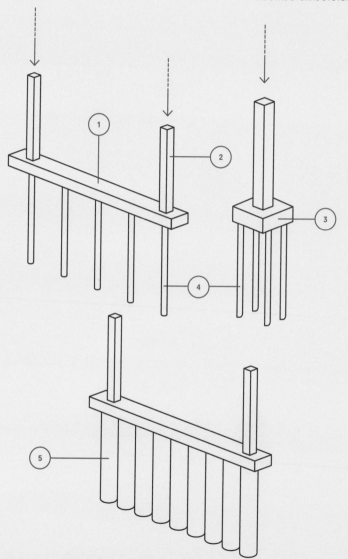

Ground-bearing Slab

A slab is a horizontal structural element of reinforced concrete. It is cast/poured on site (in-situ).

A ground-bearing slab rests on the ground as the name suggests, and is commonly used in conjunction with a strip foundation that supports the walls separately.

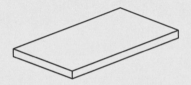

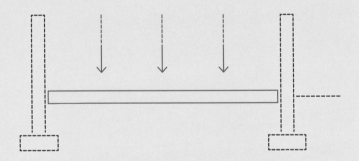

7.2.4 Retaining Walls

Retaining walls are required to hold back the ground where there is a change in level, or in basement construction. There is a tendency for the wall to overturn due to the pressure imposed on it from the ground, necessitating the 'toe' of the foundation indicated in the diagram.

There are various types of retaining walls suitable for specific construction and road-building projects.

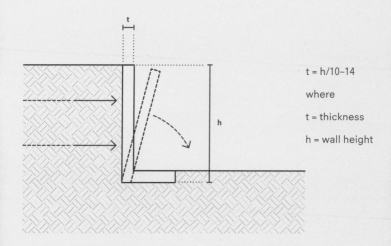

t = h/10–14

where

t = thickness

h = wall height

7.2.5 Horizontal Structural Elements

Horizontal structural elements carry the loads of floors and roofs and transfer those loads onto the vertical elements below – most commonly walls or columns.

1 Beams carry loads in a linear manner, while resisting deflection or bending. They are most commonly made from steel, concrete reinforced with steel, solid timber or glulam. The larger the span the deeper the beam needs to be to transfer the loads effectively without excessive bending.

See **Section 7.3.5** for span-to-depth ratios of steel, concrete and timber beams.

2 Joists are beams made from solid timber – see **Section 7.2.6**.

3 Slabs are typically concrete – see **Section 7.2.7**.

4 Arches – see **Section 7.2.8**.

5 Vaults – see **Section 7.2.9**.

6 Trusses – see **Section 7.2.10**.

7 Girders – see **Section 7.2.11**.

The effects of bending in a beam

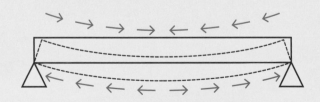

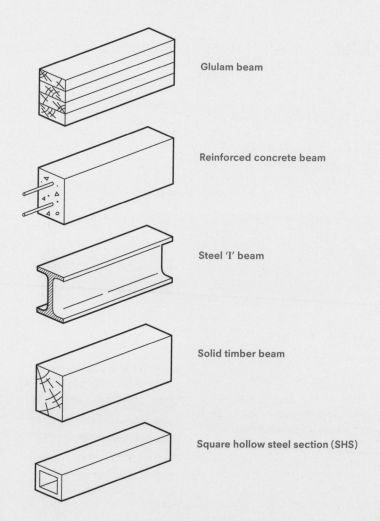

Glulam beam

Reinforced concrete beam

Steel 'I' beam

Solid timber beam

Square hollow steel section (SHS)

7.2.6 Timber Joists

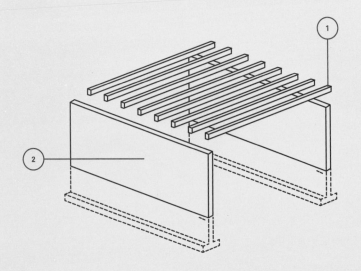

At the scale of domestic construction, it is common to use timber joists to span from one wall to another. The wall in this case can be either timber stud or masonry. The length of the span will determine the size of the joists. The joists are normally supported by the walls in this case, and will be spaced at centres of 300–600 mm (in the US 12–24") depending on the loads and the joist size and strength. Floorboards act as a secondary structural support.

NB

Loadings will vary depending on location, e.g. roof joists will normally have a smaller load than floor joists.

A span refers to the distance between two supports.

See **Section 7.3.1** for timber joist size/load spanning tables.

Fig. 127

1. Timber joist
2. Load-bearing wall

7.2.7 Concrete Slabs

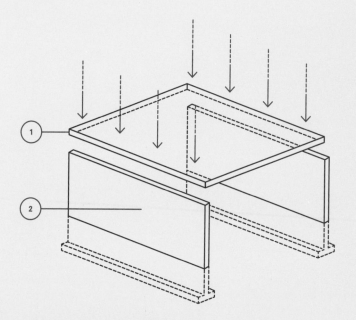

Depending on its span, a concrete slab can be simply supported, one-way spanning or two-way spanning. It can be supported by masonry or concrete walls, or by a framed structure below. Where a framed structure is used, infill walls are required.

Fig. 128

1. Concrete slab
2. Load-bearing wall

7.2.8 Arches

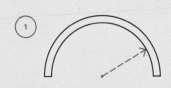

An arch is a structure that spans while also supporting weight from above.

NB
Arches are the rare horizontal structure to work for materials that are strong in compression but weak in tension (like masonry). Catenary arches – the inverted shape of a hanging rope or chain, which is formed only by the action of its own weight – are best, because when loaded, the entire arch is in pure compression.

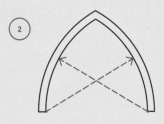

A multiple arch form will behave similarly to a barrel vault (see **Section 7.2.9**) from a structural viewpoint.

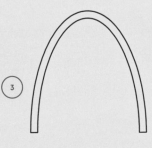

Fig. 129

1. Semicircular arch

2. Gothic arch

3. Inverted catenary arch

7.2.9 Vaults

A barrel vault can be made in brick, steel, timber or concrete – or a combination of these materials.

The vertical wall element can be replaced with a column-and-beam frame.

There is a tendency for the load on a barrel vault to cause the vault to push out sideways, so this needs to be addressed in the design of the structure. The flatter the arch, the greater the pressure.

A multiple barrel vault is possible where the base of adjoining vaults span from one support to another.

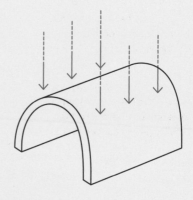

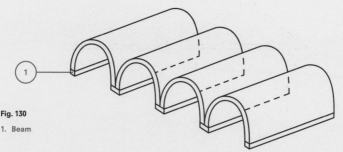

Fig. 130

1. Beam

7.2.10 Trusses

A truss is a framing device designed to span a space and to support other elements in a structure. It can be made of timber, steel or concrete. Trusses are efficient because the internal members act in pure tension, or compression, without bending.

There are multiple types of truss arrangements, with spans ranging from 5–40m (16–130'). A king post truss is shown below. Further detail is given in **Section 8.4.3**.

In domestic construction, a roof truss span is more likely to be 8–10m (26–33'). The majority of timber roof trusses used in domestic construction are prefabricated.

NB
For further information on truss types and spans, refer to Fiona Cobb, *Structural Engineer's Pocket Book* (pp. 26–27).

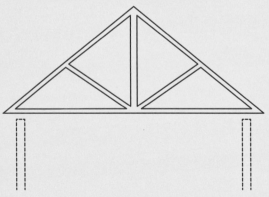

King post truss

7.2.11 Girders

A girder is a support beam made up of a framework of posts and struts. It can be made of timber, steel or concrete. Lattice girders are typically made from RSA (rolled sectional angles) or from tubular steel sections. Plate girders are made from I-sections made up of individual plates, or plates added to an existing I-section to make it stronger.

There are several different configurations possible. The example below is a Warren girder.

In the US the term 'girder' is used more widely to describe any horizontal structural element carrying other horizontal elements – the element below would be referred to as a truss.

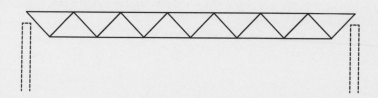

Warren girder (truss)

7.2.12 Frame Structures

A frame structure is one made from multiple rigid horizontal and vertical elements – beams, columns and slabs – which form the 'skeleton' of the building. The envelope of the building – the roof and walls – can assist in providing lateral support, but the main load-bearing elements are the rigid linear ones. Frames can be made of steel, concrete, timber or glulam and can be classified into four sub-categories:

Rigid/moment frames have fixed joints – bending is resisted within the elements.

Braced frames have added diagonal or X-shaped bracing to increase stability and resist lateral loading.

Pin-jointed frames have joints between the various rigid elements that can move or flex, so the structure gains its stability by balancing forces.

Fixed jointed frames do not allow for movement at the junctions of linear elements. Portal frames are common two-dimensional rigid frames that have the basic characteristics of a rigid joint between column and beam.

Rigid/moment frame

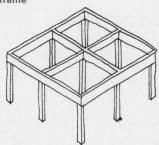

Braced frame

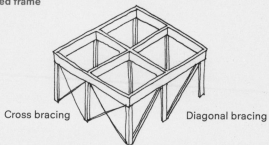

Cross bracing Diagonal bracing

Fixed jointed portal frame

Purlins for
lateral stability

Rigid joint between
column and beam

7.2.13 Shell Structures

A shell is a thin curved structure that can span large distances. The shell is typically made from concrete reinforced with steel mesh. Shell structures are lighter than alternatives and can form a simple dome or more complex curved shapes. They can be made from a singular shell or from an assembly of multiple curved surfaces. Lattice shell structures, also known as gridshells, can be used to form geodesic domes or hyperboloid domes. Shell structures are very effective at roofing large spaces.

Dome shell

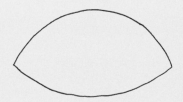

Barrell shell

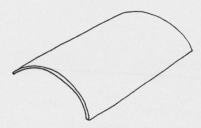

Parabolic shell

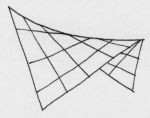

7.2.14 Tensile Structures

Tensile structures transfer loads through tension alone. Two-dimensional tensile structures include suspension bridges or cable trusses. In three-dimensional or surface tensile structures, loads are transferred across thin tensile membranes or cables. These are typically propped by compression elements such as masts or columns (like in a circus tent). They can span very large distances, so are often used in sports facilities or halls.

Cable stay bridge

Suspension bridge

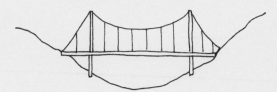

Tensile structure with and without central mast

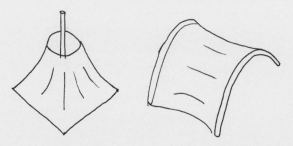

7.2.15 Space Frame Structures

Space frames are three-dimensional frameworks in which all the members are interconnected and act as a single entity, resisting loads from all directions.

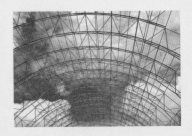

The frame is made up of top and bottom chords with diagonal chords mediating between the two.

Space frames are designed to span very large spaces.

They can also be configured to form both the roof and walls of a structure.

NB
For further information on space frame structures, refer to Andrea Deplazes, *Constructing Architecture* (p. 136).

7.2.16 Diagrid Structures

Diagrid structures comprise diagonal lattices. They are most commonly steel, but can also be made of timber or concrete. The image on the right shows the concourse roof at King's Cross station, London, by John McAslan + Partners with Arup engineers. Because diagrid structures are very effective at transferring lateral loads (such as wind loads), they are often used in high-rise construction. Diagrid structures commonly take the form of an 'exo-skeleton' wrapping the perimeter of a building and can be used for orthogonal, faceted or curved buildings. Many recent developments in skyscraper design have involved the use of exo-skeleton diagrid structures, for example the London 'Gherkin' by Foster + Partners.

7.3
Sizing of Structures

In order to design buildings, knowledge of the spans achievable with various structural systems and approximate sizes of the structural elements is key to making feasible proposals. In this section we set out some rules of thumb for common structural elements and give tables for sizing timber and glulam beams.

7.3.1 Timber Joists

Timber floors or roofs are constructued with closely spaced, parallel timber beams called joists. Joists are classified by their depth and strength.

The joists span from one support to another. These supports can be either masonry or timber walls, or a beam. As well as end support, joists will require what is known as lateral support. This is the introduction of intermediate stiffening elements between joists, known as strutting or blocking.

Additional strength also comes from the sheet or board covering fixed to the top of the joists.

The spacing of joists from centre to centre (c/c) ranges from 300 to 600 mm. In the US the range is 12"–24" but 16" is the standard. Traditionally, floor boarding required closer spacing, in the region of 400mm c/c, but the increased use of sheet-material flooring commonly allows for spacing of joists at 600 mm c/c (in the US 16" is standard).

As with all floors, they must support their own weight (dead load) and the load that will be imposed on them. The extent of this live load will depend on the building's use.

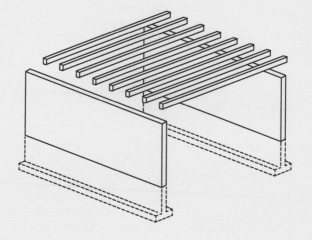

In summary, the strength of timber-joist floors and roofs will be determined by:

- their span
- the spacing of joists
- the strength of timber used
- the flooring surface they are fixed to
- the loading on the floor/roof.

For architect, it is helpful to be able to estimate the size and spacing of joists in the early stages of design to more accurately develop a design.

With this in mind, on the opposite page we have included a span table for guidance on joist sizes relative to their proposed span. Imposed loads and dead loads are also indicated.

In public buildings, the loadings can be as much as three times the load for domestic situations. Because of the greater spans involved in larger buildings, joists start to become unworkable at this scale.

In order to span greater lengths in timber, engineered timbers are required.

NB
All sizing tables in this section are for preliminary design guideline purposes only.

In the US, a useful table can be found at **www.southernpine.com/app/uploads/SPtable2_060113.pdf**

Size (mm)	Strength Class A			Strength Class B			Strength Class C		
	300	400	600	300	400	600	300	400	600
44 × 100	2.19	1.98	1.66	2.29	2.08	1.81	2.39	2.16	1.89
44 × 115	2.52	2.28	1.89	2.63	2.39	2.07	2.74	2.48	2.16
44 × 125	2.74	2.48	2.05	2.87	2.59	2.25	2.98	2.71	2.35
44 × 150	3.28	2.98	2.43	3.44	3.12	2.72	3.58	3.25	2.83
44 × 175	3.84	3.45	2.82	4.02	3.65	3.16	4.18	3.79	3.30
44 × 200	4.38	3.92	3.20	4.59	4.16	3.62	4.78	4.33	3.77
44 × 225	4.94	4.38	3.57	5.17	4.69	4.08	5.38	4.88	4.24
75 × 150	3.94	3.58	3.11	4.12	3.74	3.26	4.29	3.89	3.40
75 × 175	4.60	4.17	3.63	4.81	4.37	3.80	5.01	4.54	3.96
75 × 225	5.91	5.37	4.67	6.19	5.61	4.89	6.44	5.84	5.09

Fig. 131

Span tables for timber joists

The table above indicates the permissible span (in metres) of various sizes of joist in relation to the spacing of joists (in millimetres), and assumes a domestic loading of: imposed load of 1.5 kN/m² and dead load of 0.25 kN/m².

For residential construction in the US the norm is 40 psf for live loads and 10 psf for dead loads.

The joist sizes are the minimum permissible sizes at 22% moisture content. The permissible span is the clear span between supports.

NB Where joists span distances of greater than 2.5 m (8') strutting is used to prevent the joists from twisting. See **Section 8.2.9**.

7.3.2 Engineered Timber Beams

When a required floor span is no longer feasible with ordinary timber joists, a number of engineered timber alternatives are available.

Glulam Beams
Glulam beams are an economical way of spanning longer distances in timber. Regular 'off the shelf' glulam beams come in standard, stock dimensions of up to 20 m/60' (depending on the manufacturer). However, larger sizes – up to 50 m (164') – can be ordered. Transport, from the factory to the site, can be difficult with larger beams. Glulam beams and columns are connected with steel elements. They are designed as engineered, laminated structural components. Structural glulam elements are made by bonding together accurately planed timber strips, with their grain in the longitudinal direction of the member. This forms a structural unit of great strength and dimensional stability.

One of the great advantages of glulam is that it can be curved and formed to a variety of shapes to suit different structural and design requirements.

Glulam can be used for arches, portal frames and floor beams, columns, rafters and A-frames, purlins and joists.

Please refer to **Section 6.3.13** for standard glulam sizes available.

For further information, see:
www.glulambeams.co.uk

Fig. 132

Glulam beam

7.3.3 **Ply-webbed Beams**

The structural advantage of ply-webbed beams comes from the use of plywood as a shear-resistant material.

The result is a saving of material: a stiffer, lighter beam than other timber solutions for the same span/loads. This makes ply-webbed beams an economical alternative.

Ply-webbed beams are used for larger spans in the region of 12–15m (40–50'), where solid timber is not a feasible or realistic option. They allow greater spanning distances with less beam/floor depth.

The web part of the beam can be replaced with a steel lattice, making a composite timber-and-steel beam. The advantage of this is that services can pass through the voids in the lattice part of the beam.

Fig. 133

1. Ply-webbed beams
2. Solid timber element
3. Plywood sheeting

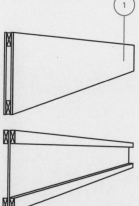

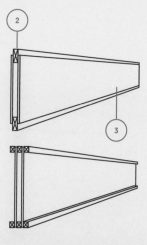

7.3.4 Concrete Framed Structures

When it comes to RC (reinforced concrete) frames, there are a number of rules of thumb that can be helpful in the early stages of design to assist in calculating basic spans and slab thicknesses.

A framed structure usually implies the use of a structural grid. The grid is overlaid on each plan level to align structural elements that repeat from floor to floor. It also assists greatly when it comes to setting out a building on site, as it allows for easy coordination of dimensions. A grid of 5–6 m (c.16–20') is a good start for setting out a concrete framed structure

NB
Where a structural grid is used, it will have implications for the layout of rooms and walls.

Lift Core
A solid structural element inserted into the structural grid, typically cast in-situ concrete. The lift core can contribute to the stiffness of the overall structure.

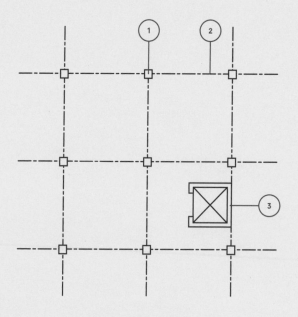

Fig. 134

Structural grid

1. Column

2. Grid line

3. Lift core

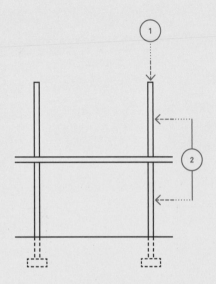

Alignment of Columns

Generally, columns are in the same position in plan from one floor to the next, as this allows a direct transfer of forces to the foundations.

Columns are more economical when they are constructed to the same size.

A structural grid allows for clear setting out of columns and other structural elements.

Fig. 135

Structural grid

1. Forces
2. Alignment

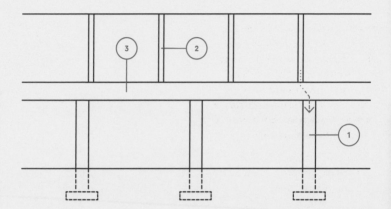

Transfer Slab

A transfer slab can be introduced where a complete change of column grid layout is required on an upper level. The thickness of the transfer slab allows for the changing location of column loads, as the loads are transferred within the depth of the slab.

A transfer slab is commonly used between basement and ground-floor level where the floor layout above is significantly different.

Other transfer structures include beams and trusses.

Fig. 136

1. Column grid A
2. Column grid B
3. Transfer slab

445

7.3.5 Span-to-depth Ratios

Span-to-depth ratios provide rules of thumb for preliminary sizing of structural elements, but should be used with caution because they assume standard loads. They are still a useful tool in the early stages of design in estimating the sizes of various structural solutions.

To calculate what the appropriate size of a glulam beam would be for a building span of 10 m:

Span: 10m ÷ 17 (halfway between 15 and 20 as noted in the table opposite) = 0.58 m

To calculate the same span 10 m using a ribbed slab:

Span: 10 m ÷ 37 = 0.27 m

For concrete elements with steel reinforcement, 50–75 mm can be presumed as appropriate cover.

When working in I-P units, the principle is the same.

NB

For more graphic representations of span-to-depth ratios, we recommend *The Architect's Studio Companion* by Edward Allen and Joseph Iano, and *Building Structures Illustrated* by Francis Ching et al.

Span Tables for Common Structural Elements

Elements L is the length of the span (assuming beams are simply supported at each end)	Typical Span Metric	Similar I-P Units	Span-to-depth Ratio
STEEL			
Universal beam (I beam) – heavy or point loading	4–12 m	10'–40'	L/10–15
Universal beam (I beam) – light distributed loading	4–12 m	10'–40'	L/15–25
Cantilever beam	0–5 m	0–16'	L/1–7
Castellated beams	4–12 m	10'–40'	L/10–15
Lattice roof girders	5–20 m	16'–65'	L/12–15
Portal frames	10–60 m	30'–200'	L/35–40
Space frames	10–	30'–320'	L/15–30
CONCRETE			
One-way spanning concrete slab	5–6 m	16'–20'	L/28–36
Two-way spanning concrete slab	6–11 m	20'–36'	L/24–35
Flat slab	4–8 m	10'–26'	L/27
Ribbed slab (ribs at 900–1500 mm c/c)	6–11 m	20'–36'	L/35–40
Waffle slab	8–15 m	26'–50'	L/18–20
Rectangular reinforced beams	3–10 m	10'–30'	L/20
TIMBER			
Softwood timber-joist flooring	2–5 m	6'–16'	L/10–20
Glulam beam	5–20 m	16'–65'	L/15–20
Ply-web beam	5–20 m	16'–65'	L/10–15

7.4
The Potential of Structure

For architects, it is relevant to consider the design of buildings as an all-encompassing process. This is also true when it comes to the structures that hold up our buildings. To this end, we must always seek out the potential that structure can provide, so that we can exploit it where possible and allow it to reinforce and/ or represent an architectural idea in context. The house illustrated on the following pages is an inspiring example of how structural design can enhance architectural design.

7.4.1 **Larger Structural Elements**

Photo courtesy
of Ros Kavanagh

Hall House, designed by Grafton Architects in 1999, is a three-storey house located in Dublin.

It occupies a corner infill site, and is read externally as a brick box with a separate layer of stone wall.

It has been described as a house where corners never meet; this theme is made explicit by the inventive use of structure between the external and internal living spaces at first-floor level.

Project referenced with the kind permission of Grafton Architects

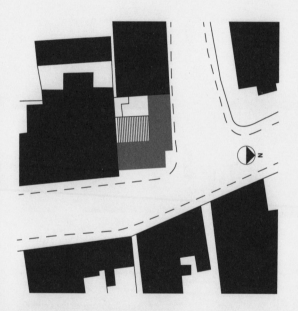

Because the site is located on the northeastern corner of an urban block, and in order to take advantage of the best light, the accommodation is stacked and pushed to the outer edges of the site, creating a stepped void of courtyards and terraces that relate to the interior at all three levels.

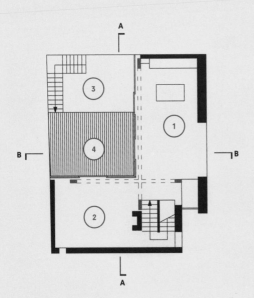

First floor plan

1. Dining/Kitchen
2. Living
3. Entrance courtyard below
4. Decked terrace

At first-floor level, the main living spaces surround and open onto a terrace decked in timber, which is reached by stairs from the lower entrance court.

The connected nature of these two internal and external living spaces is reinforced and delicately held by the structural form, which can be clearly read in the living spaces.

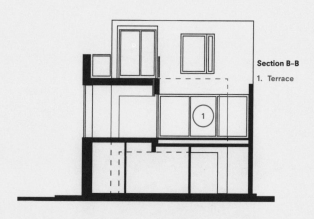

Section B–B

1. Terrace

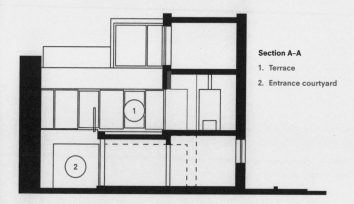

Section A–A

1. Terrace

2. Entrance courtyard

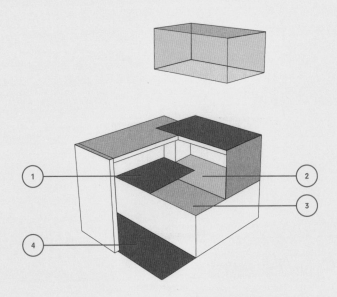

First floor plan

1. Dining/Kitchen
2. Living
3. Decked court
4. External access courtyard

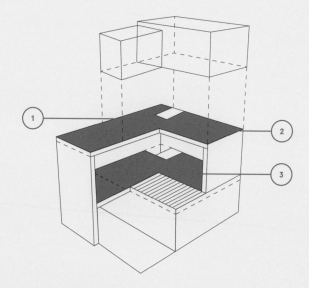

Because of the L-shaped form of the living spaces, the concrete slab overhead requires support along its edges.

This is easily achieved on the outer edges of the slab, as the load-bearing walls carry the slab along that edge.

Fig. 137

Floor slabs to be supported in red

1. Outer edge of slab carried by load-bearing walls here
2. Ceiling slab of first-floor living spaces
3. Floor slab of first-floor living spaces

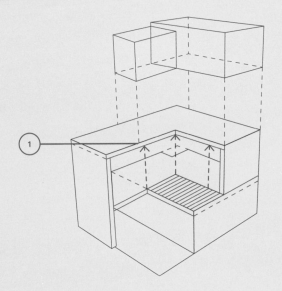

Fig. 138

1. Inner edge requiring support

Along the inner edges of the L-shaped slab, however, it is difficult to achieve support as the slab spans are significant and the slab will require continuous support along both lengths.

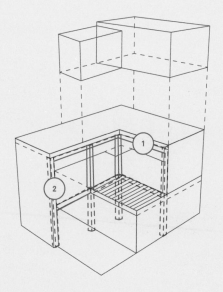

A typical structural solution that is commonly proposed is a framed structure of columns and beams (as indicated above) with a downstand beam providing the continuous support.

A downstand beam in this instance would probably be about 250–300mm (10–12″) in depth.

Fig. 139

1. Downstand beam
2. Column framework

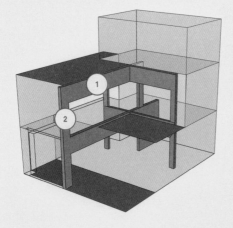

Fig. 140

1. Downstand beam
2. Column framework

The actual solution adopted uses a concrete structure, also with a downstand beam. However, because the beam depth is increased to 1m this allows the columns to be pushed further back from the corner junction. The beam's greater depth allows a larger span between columns. The columns are also lengthened in one direction.

The deep beam is held back from the external wall, which allows the structure to read independently.

Because there is no column at the corner where the beams cross, this allows the space to open up internally and connect with the external terrace, reinforcing the architectural concept.

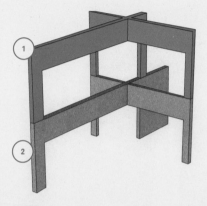

The diagram above shows the first-floor structure in red, with the supporting ground-floor structure in grey underneath, viewed from the soutwest.

Fig. 141

1. First-floor structure
2. Ground floor structure

1

2

Structure in context – view from
dining room (terrace to the right).

Fig. 142

1. Position of structure in living area
2. Terrace

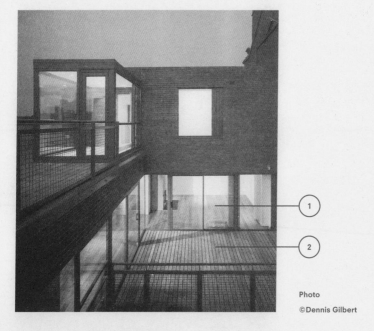

Photo
©Dennis Gilbert

Structure in context – external view at night from second-floor level.

The concept of the house as a place where the corners never meet is further reinforced by the glass-to-glass corner junction where a column has been 'removed'.

Fig. 143

1. Living area
2. External terrace

461

8

Principles of Construction

Construction is the mother tongue
of the architect. The architect is
a poet who thinks and speaks in
terms of construction.
—Auguste Perret

From an architect's point of view, an understanding of how buildings were made, how they are made today and how they could be made in the future underpins the conceptual design, organization, planning and development of a building.

The design strategy, structural systems and materials you choose will influence the expression, sustainability and feasibility of your buildings, but, most importantly, the impact of these decisions needs to be understood from an environmental point of view.

In this chapter we discuss the principles of domestic-scale construction, past and present, beginning with the 'rules of thumb' that explain the primary functions of building. We go on to illustrate the composition of two common building systems – masonry and timber frame – by looking at the build-up and function of the primary elements of construction: floors, walls and roofs. We also look at some ways of forming openings and junctions.

As new materials and systems are continuously evolving, our aim is to encourage an understanding of construction from first principles. This understanding will allow you the freedom to be innovative and experimental in your approach to architectural design and technology – core skills for an architect.

Primary functions

Building methods have evolved over time, so it is helpful to look back and see where current building practice has come from in order to understand why we build the way we do.

Historically, buildings have been constructed from homogeneous materials at a slow pace and to well-known familiar details using traditional techniques. This knowledge was passed on from generation to generation as construction methods evolved.

In contrast to this, in the last 100 years or so innovation in relation to materials, processes and forms of construction has accelerated at an ever-increasing rate, leading to the need for a different approach.

The rapid expansion of new technologies has meant radical changes in how we build and increased levels of complexity in the process and compilation of building. An increased awareness of environmental implications has led to a rise in performance standards required of the building envelope.

Traditional details have been modified or fundamentally re-thought to fulfil these new and ever-changing building performance standards.

These advancements present an opportunity for the architect, who, with a sound understanding of the principles of construction, can find new and inventive ways to build.

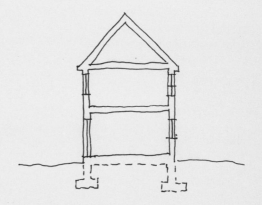

Building envelope

The building envelope is the part
of a building that separates the
internal environment from the
external environment, and is made
up of the floor, walls and roof.

To guide you in your understanding of the functions of the building envelope, it is helpful to think of some 'rules of thumb', which require the building to:

- stand up
- stay warm
- stay dry
- breathe
- contain well-considered junctions
- be beautiful.

As you design and draw your own technical details, use this checklist to understand what each element is doing:

- What's carrying the load?
- What's keeping the building warm?
- What's keeping it dry?
- How is the building breathing (how is moisture and air moving through the fabric of the building envelope)?

It's also important to consider how elements are joined. Different materials move and react differently, which is often the source of problems.

These functions need to be achieved within a framework of regional or national building regulations and compliance. You need to be aware of building systems and methods of construction that are particular to your local climate, the availability of materials and local skill levels.

Further reading

Constructing Architecture: Materials, Processes, Structures (2008) by Andrea Deplazes is a very good overall construction book.

The Environmental Design Pocket Book, 2nd Edition (2015) by Sofie Pelsmakers

A Visual Dictionary of Architecture (2011) by Francis D.K. Ching

Introduction to Architectural Technology, 3rd Edition (2021) by Pete Silver and Will McLean

101 Rules of Thumb for Low Energy Architecture (2013) by Huw Heywood

Make it stand up

Junctions are critical

Stay dry

Be beautiful! ♥

Let it breathe

Definitions

Build-up
Refers to the differing materials that make up a wall, floor or roof construction and the order in which they are placed, from inside to outside.

Composite
Composite refers to elements made up of more than one material. An example would be an alu-clad window, which is made up of aluminium cladding on the exterior, wood on the interior and glazing between. It is known as a composite window.

Thermal Insulation
A means of maintaining the internal temperature of a building by providing a layer of insulating material in which heat flow is reduced.

Cold Bridge/Thermal Bridge
One of the principles of modern construction is to provide a continuous layer of thermal insulation throughout the external layer of the building. Where the insulation layer is broken by a non-insulating material, it has bridged the insulation layer – hence the term 'cold bridge'.

Breather Membrane
The purpose of a breather membrane is to allow water vapour from within the building fabric to escape, while also preventing water from entering the building fabric from the outside.

Vapour Barrier
A plastic or foil sheet that resists the passage of moisture through a wall, ceiling or floor.

R-Value and U-Value
Insulating materials are assigned a quantitative measure of their insulating capability, known as a R-value. The R-value is a measure of a material's ability to resist heat flow, which will vary depending on the thickness and type of that material. The higher the R-value the greater is the resistance to heat flow.

The U-Value of a building element is the sum of all the R-values of each material, inverted (1/R-values). The lower the U-value the better able the building fabric is to retain heat. All buildings will lose heat over time, but the wall, floor and roof build-up will determine the rate at which the heat will be lost. The thermal-insulation layer plays a big part in this.

Flashing
A thin, continuous piece of sheet metal or other impervious material installed to prevent water entering a structure through an angle or joint.

Weep Holes
Small openings left in the outer wall of masonry construction to allow water inside a building to move outside the wall.

Leaf
An outer or inner wall in a cavity or sandwich panel-wall build-up.

Weathering
The aging and decay of building materials due to exposure to the environment and weather.

8.1
Constructing the Dwelling

From the prehistoric age human shelters have been made from the materials to hand. Available materials vary from place to place for reasons to do with climate and geology. Even so, it can be seen that the same principles of construction apply.

In this prehistoric hut, timber poles are driven into the ground in an oval layout allowing space for the entrance. More poles are tied to the ground poles and fastened together at the top (critical junctions). This forms the main structure and makes the hut stand up.

The covering of reed thatch keeps it warm and dry, and lets it breathe.

The form and materials used make it beautiful!

Fig. 144

Prehistoric thatched hut

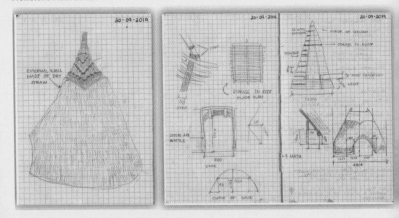

8.1.1 Masonry

Masonry is 'the art and craft of building and fabricating in stone, clay, brick or concrete block. Construction of poured concrete, reinforced or unreinforced, is often also considered masonry.'
Encyclopedia Britannica

Domestic masonry vernacular construction has a long history throughout Europe, Asia, Africa and the Americas. The British Isles has a long tradition of constructing vernacular buildings in the countryside, where, prior to the Industrial Revolution, most people lived. These small, single-storey houses were usually one room deep and made from local materials. In Ireland and Britain this usually meant stone and earth walls, with a lime plaster applied externally to protect the walls from weathering while also allowing them to breathe. The roof was of timber construction and commonly covered with thatch or sod. Floors were initally compacted earth, later covered in flagstones.

With the development of towns and cities in the eighteenth and nineteenth centuries, it became possible and necessary to build taller and more densely. Brick and stone had been used to construct buildings for thousands of years, but improvements in quality and the ability to mass-produce brick during the Industrial Revolution provided an alternative to the traditional single-storey dwelling construction method.

Fig. 145

Simple masonry/earth construction with timber pitched roof.

471

This technological advance is demonstrated by the evolution of the townhouse.

The walls of these houses were built of solid masonry, usually a combination of brick and stone, which was held together with lime mortar. Floors and roofs were of timber construction with slate pitched-roof finishes. As the quality and consistency of brick production improved it began to be used on the front elevation.

These buildings were designed to breathe, but this led to other problems. The porous nature of brick allowed wind-driven rain to penetrate into their interiors, causing damp and decay to the timbers and fine finishes inside. In the mid-1800s an early version of the 'cavity wall' was introduced to remedy this. Creating a cavity in a wall involves building two walls beside each other, separated by a gap, but with both leaves tied together. The outer wall and cavity provide a moisture barrier, keeping the inner wall dry. This solution is best suited to damp climates.

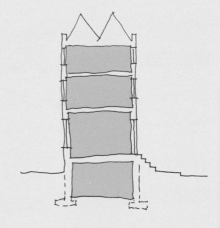

Fig. 146

Typical townhouse section.

These drawings show how cavity walls were tied together with bricks initially and then later with iron wall ties. The cavity performed a number of functions:

- It prevented water and condensation from reaching the interior.
- It allowed the water and vapour that penetrated the outer leaf to dry out.
- It allowed the building to breathe (air to move between the inside and outside).

In the bottom diagram, the inner leaf is structural, the outer layer is dealing with moisture. The cavity, combined with the mass of the brick, form the thermal envelope.

This type of construction developed and became mainstream for the best part of the twentieth century in Europe and, later, North America.

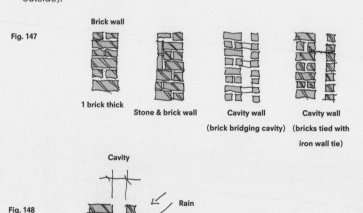

Fig. 147

Brick wall

1 brick thick

Stone & brick wall

Cavity wall
(brick bridging cavity)

Cavity wall
(bricks tied with
iron wall tie)

Fig. 148

Cavity

Inside

Rain

Breathable wall

Vapour barrier

Further developments in concrete block production made for an economical alternative to brick. The block wall could be rendered externally with sand and cement, which acts as a waterproof layer. This was followed by the hollow block/cavity block method, in which a single block containing an air cavity replaced the need for an inner and outer leaf, and was rendered externally.

The older and thicker solid walls of previous centuries had good thermal mass, but the cavity and hollow block walls of more recent times were poor at retaining heat. As a result these building are expensive to heat, requiring the burning of excessive amounts of fossil fuel that damage the environment. Changes in building regulations gave rise to the use of thermal insulation within the wall build-up to address this issue, and traditional construction methods were adapted to include it.

A further development is the hollow clay block, which forms a solid wall construction and has good thermal properties owing to the air trapped inside the voids of the block. Steel and concrete are also used in residential construction, but to a lesser extent (**See Section 7.4**).

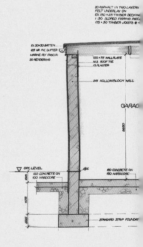

Fig. 149

Typical section through a 1980s cavity-wall house.

Courtesy Cormac Allen

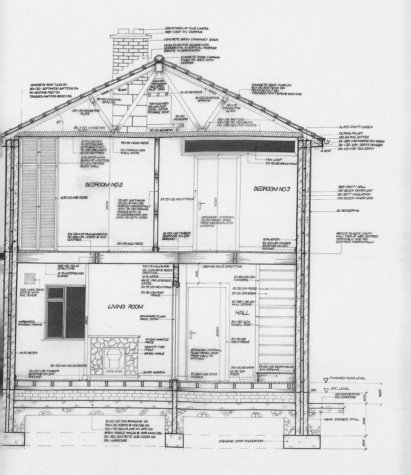

8.1.2 Timber

Building in timber dates back to prehistoric times, using methods that involve both solid timber construction and 'green' timber-framed structures clad in various natural materials like reeds or straw. Green timber has not been seasoned – i.e. it still contains a high percentage of moisture.

Today there are two main construction types that are commonplace in timber building systems: 'post and beam' and 'platform frame'.

Modern advances in technology have led to the production of factory-made platform-frame

timber components. This method of construction lends itself to off-site prefabrication of walls; floors; room pods; and, in some instances, whole house assemblies.

Cross-laminated timber (CLT) is another form of platform-frame timber construction in which walls, floors and roofs are pre-formed out of solid engineered wood and assembled on site. As timber is a renewable resource, it is more environmentally friendly than standard masonry construction.

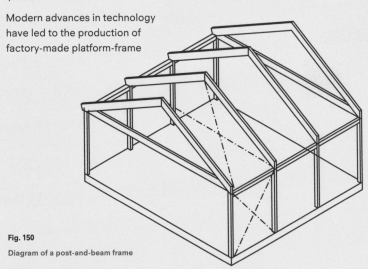

Fig. 150

Diagram of a post-and-beam frame

With post-and-beam construction, the structural loads are carried by vertical (posts) and horizontal (beams) timber elements (Fig. 150). These elements canbe either solid or laminated (see **Section 6.3.13** for sizes of laminated glulam elements).

Using solid timber has limitations in terms of the loads that can be carried and the spacing between vertical posts. In the case of post-and-beam construction, the infill walls are non-load-bearing between the structural elements – unlike platform-frame construction, in which the walls themselves perform a structural role.

Platform frame construction (Fig. 151) allows a building to be made up in panels that act structurally and fit together. The wall panels are continuous from floor to ceiling and perform a structural role, carrying the loads of the intermediate floors and roof.

NB
See **Section 7.3.2** for information about engineered timber elements used in timber-framed construction today.

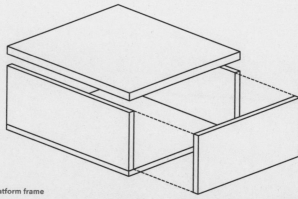

Fig. 151
Diagram of a platform frame

8.2
Floors

Floors can be divided into two categories: ground and upper floors.

Ground floors must:

- keep the heat in and the cold out (in warmer climates, the opposite is the case – floors must keep heat out)
- be able to withstand the loads bearing on them (dead and live loads)
- prevent the growth of organic matter up through the floor plate
- protect the interior of the building against moisture penetration from the ground
- provide a safe and comfortable finish on which to walk.

Ground floors below the external ground level, including basement floors, are not covered here. For further information on basement construction, refer to Andrea Deplazes, *Constructing Architecture* (pp. 153–161).

While issues to do with moisture penetration and organic growth are not relevant on upper floors, a number of other concerns arise.

Upper floors should:

- resist the spread of fire between levels
- provide sound insulation.

Upper floors may also be designed to accommodate services – pipes, cables, wiring, etc.

All floors, ground and upper, should be durable enough to withstand expected wear and tear.

8.2.1 Ground-floor Slab

The most common floor is a concrete cast in-situ steel-reinforced slab. Cast in-situ is concrete that is poured on site into a mould. Precast concrete arrives already cast and set, and is used where the ground needs to be spanned.

Cast concrete is widely used in domestic and larger-scale construction. The concrete is cast into a mould on a layer of hardcore (compressed rubble and gravel) or on rigid insulation.

Typically a concrete cast in-situ slab is around 150 mm (6") deep.

Fig. 152

1. Insulation
2. Concrete slab
3. Hardcore
4. DPM/Radon barrier

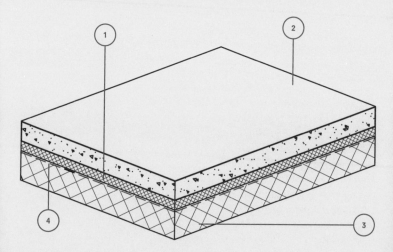

A cast in-situ concrete slab must also include a damp-proof membrane (DPM), which prevents water from penetrating through the slab. The DPM is usually a heavy-duty plastic or polythene sheet. Care must be taken when this is laid to ensure that it is not pierced or damaged by the hardcore, or this may result in water infiltration. This DPM can also function as a radon barrier. Radon is a naturally occurring radioactive gas, which can cause lung cancer when allowed to build up in internal environments. For more information on radon, its effects and how to reduce risk, refer to the Environmental Protection Agency of Ireland (www.epa.ie/radon), the UK Society for Radiological Protection (www.srp-uk.org), or the US Environmental Protection Agency (www.epa.gov/radon). To avoid piercing the radon barrier/DPM with the hardcore or rough concrete slab, a thin layer of sand ('sand blinding') is added between.

Finally, most cast in-situ floors are finished with a screed. The screed is a thin layer of finer concrete than the slab itself. This can be exposed in the finished internal floor or can provide a level base for alternative floor finishes such as tiles, carpet, etc.

The screed is typically 75mm (3") thick, but specialist screeds can be laid to 50mm (2") and can include underfloor heating if required. Their composition allows for a more rapid transfer of heat.

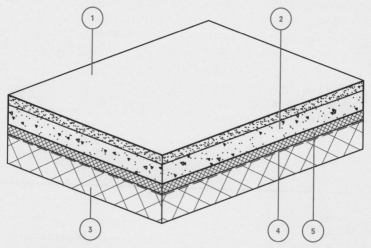

Fig. 153

1. Concrete screed
2. Concrete slab
3. Hardcore
4. DPM/radon barrier
5. Insulation

8.2.2 Typical Ground-floor Slab

A common floor build-up is where a concrete screed is separated from the slab by the insulation and the DPM. The insulation is protected against moisture penetration as the DPM stops any moisture rising from the ground before it comes into contact with the insulation and screed.

The screed in this build-up is known as a 'floating screed' because it is said to 'float' on the insulation.

An advantage of this build-up is that internal spaces heat up more quickly, as the screed is thinner than a full slab and so does not absorb a large amount of heat. This build-up is often used with underfloor heating, as the insulation 'reflects' the heat back into the room.

Fig. 154

1. Concrete screed
2. Insulation

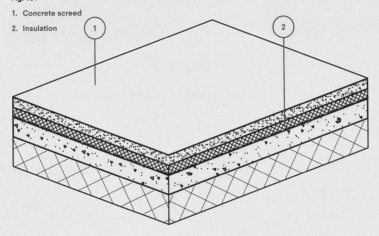

8.2.3 Suspended Ground Floor

Fig. 155

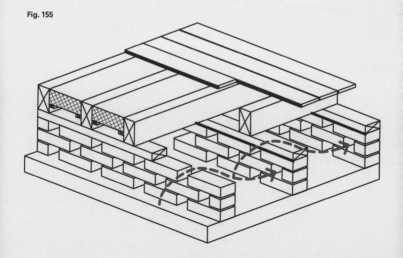

8.2.4 Insulated Floor Slab and Foundation

Constantly rising standards in the thermal-performance requirements of the building fabric have given rise to better forms of building construction. As well as reducing the heat flow through the building structure, a well-insulated and sustainably constructed building fabric means lower CO_2 emissions and less need for heating as we move towards carbon-neutral building. This floor system means less concrete is used, resulting in a lower carbon footprint and eliminating the cold bridge at the junction of the wall and floor.

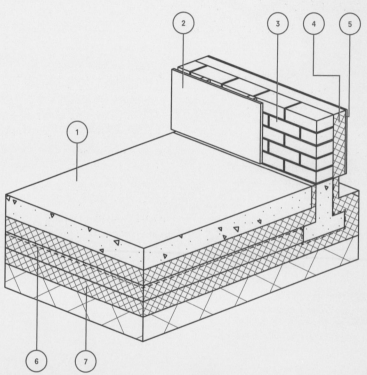

Fully insulated wall and floor

Fig. 156

1. Slab
2. Internal lining
3. Solid block wall
4. External insulation
5. External render
6. DPM/Radon barrier
7. Expanded polystyrene
   foam (EPS) insulation

8.2.5 Full-fill Cavity with Insulated Foundation

The benefit of an insulated foundation when combined with a cavity wall is that it eliminates any cold bridge at the critical junction of the wall and the floor, something that is a lot more difficult to do with a conventional strip foundation.

However, because the foundation for the outer and inner walls are separate there is a risk of differential settlement, making an engineer's approval of the foundation detailing used here critical.

It may not be possible to use this method because it will also be dependent on the bearing capacity of the soil.

The diagram here is for illustrative purposes only.

Fig. 157

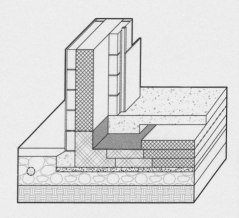

Fig. 158

1. External render
2. External block leaf
3. Full-fill cavity insulation
4. Internal block leaf
5. Airtight membrane
6. Service cavity
7. Internal wall finish
8. DPM
9. DPC
10. Foundation

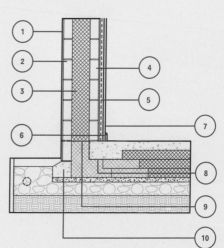

8.2.6 Timber-framed Wall and Insulated Foundation

Because of its sustainable credentials, timber is a very viable option for domestic construction. Its assembly also makes it easier to achieve a zero carbon footprint, depending on the timber source and types and amount of insulation used.

The example shown here achieves thermal continuity by connecting the external insulation layer with the foundation insulation. Moisture and radon gas are kept out by the radon/DPM layer shown in red.

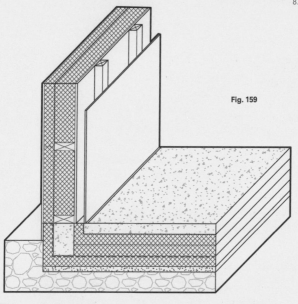

Fig. 159

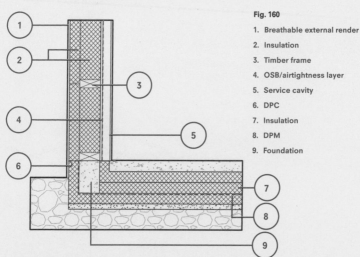

Fig. 160

1. Breathable external render
2. Insulation
3. Timber frame
4. OSB/airtightness layer
5. Service cavity
6. DPC
7. Insulation
8. DPM
9. Foundation

8.2.7 Upper Floors

Upper floors must span between load-bearing elements (see **Chapter 7** for more information on spans). Floors can be supported on load-bearing walls or structural frames. The following are types of upper floors.

Cast In-situ Concrete Floors
These are not commonly used in domestic construction. Labour-intensive, they are capable of forming complex shapes.

Precast Concrete Slabs
These smaller, factory-made slabs lie side by side and span between structural elements.

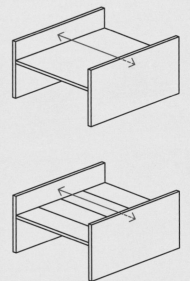

Timber Joists

This is the most common form of domestic construction for upper floor levels. Closely spaced timber joists span from wall to wall. Suitable for both masonry and timber-framed wall construction.

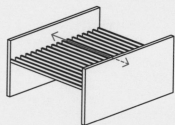

Frame Structure

When constructing upper-level floors, decking elements span between beams that are supported on columns. The frame structure may be made of timber, steel or concrete.

These decking elements can be constructed of timber (such as plywood or other processed sheet timber), precast concrete slabs, metal or composite panels of metal and concrete.

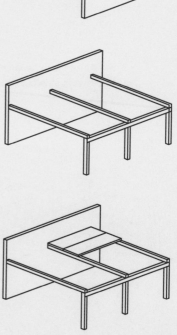

8.2.8 Timber-joist Upper Floors

In houses, upper floors are typically constructed from timber joists, spanning between structural walls. Common timber joist sizes are 50 × 225mm and 75 × 250mm, and are spaced at 400–600mm centres. In the US, common sizes are 2 × 10" and 2 × 12". Spacing is typically 16" c/c. (but could range from 12" to 24"). A timber-joist floor can span up to 6m (19'-8") depending on the dimensions, spacing of joists and the loads.

The joists are typically connected to (and supported off) blockwork walls by joist hangers. These are folded metal 'shoes', which hold the joists in place and are bedded into the mortar layers in the blockwork courses.

Plasterboard is often fixed below the joists to form the ceiling, and floorboards or sheet decking above to form the floor finish.

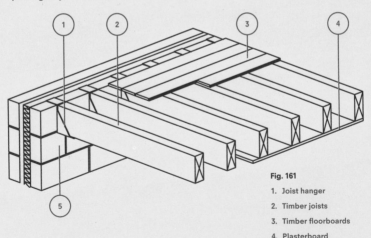

Fig. 161

1. Joist hanger
2. Timber joists
3. Timber floorboards
4. Plasterboard
5. Cavity wall

8.2.9 Strutting/Blocking

Where joists have to span distances of greater than 2.5 m (8′), strutting (bracing) is used to prevent the joists from twisting along their lengths, thereby strengthening the floor.

Strutting should be placed at 1.25 m (4′) centres along the span length and can be solid pieces of timber or diagonal timber battens (called 'herringbone strutting'). Galvanized metal strutting is also an option, allowing services to pass through.

Fig. 162

1. Herringbone strutting
2. Solid blocking

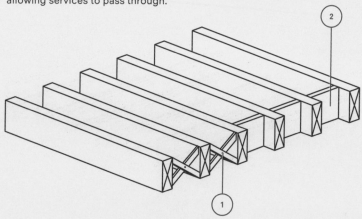

8.2.10 Engineered Joists

To span greater distances than
solid timber allows (up to 6
metres) engineered joists can
be used at the domestic scale.
These trusses have been designed
to be lighter and stronger than
solid timber. Three main types
are commonly used: I joists,
metal-web joists and LVL joists
(laminated veneered lumber).

Fig. 163

1. I joist

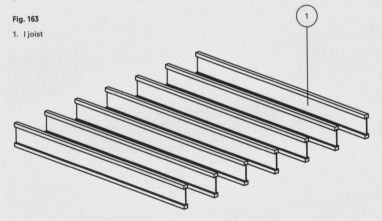

8.2.11 Composite Floors

This type of flooring has the advantage of allowing services (e.g. wires, pipes) to run within the metal profiles.

It is commonly used in medium-scale commercial or industrial applications and in large-scale construction. It is unusual in domestic construction.

Fig. 164

1. Steel reinforcement
2. Reinforced concrete
3. Profiled metal sheeting

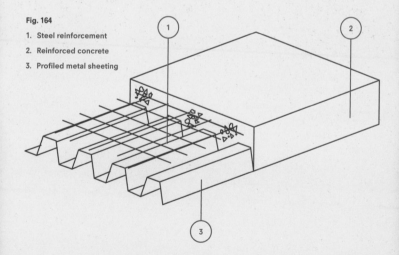

8.3
Walls

The role of the wall in building is six-fold. It must:

- carry loads
- keep the heat in and the cold out (or vice versa)
- control air movement
- minimize the passage of sound
- resist the spread of fire
- protect the building against moisture movement.

As well as these technical requirements, a wall should be considered from an aesthetic point of view in the context of the overall design.

8.3.1 Solid Masonry Walls

Traditionally, walls were made of solid construction, generally from a combination of masonry (stone, brick, earth) and mortar. They may have been finished externally with a lime-based render.

Today solid walls are achieved in a variety of different ways.

Commonly the modern composition of the solid wall is block, with an external layer of insulation finished with an acrylic render. External insulation increases the building's ability to retain heat, which means that it requires less energy to heat for the same amount of time than it would have traditionally. External insulation allows for easier thermal junctions at openings and reduces the likelihood of cold bridges.

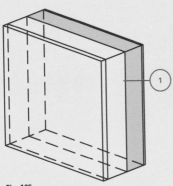

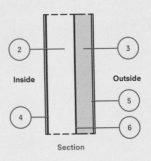

Inside   Outside

Section

Fig. 165

1. 3D view

2. Load-bearing wall keeps it up

3. External insulation keeps it warm

4. Internal lining

5. External render keeps it dry

6. Airtight layer

8.3.2 Cavity Walls

In Irish domestic construction in the twentieth century, the enclosing wall tended to have a 'cavity wall' build-up.

In cavity walls, the inner leaf typically acts structurally but both leaves are tied together at points for stability using wall tiles.

In order to comply with building standards full-fill cavity insulation is used with a minimum thickness of 140mm (5 ½") in a cavity of 150mm (6").

This wall type has been commonly used in domestic construction one to three storeys high. The inner leaf can vary in width from 100 to 215mm (4–8 ½") depending on the plan layout, number of storeys and the structural requirements of the design.

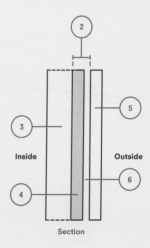

Fig. 166

1. 3D view
2. Cavity provides separation
3. Inner wall/leaf keeps it up
4. Location of insulation keeps it warm
5. Outer wall/leaf keeps it dry
6. Air gap lets it breathe

Inside

Outside

Section

NB
Although cavity-wall construction is still used today, more energy-efficient construction systems (including timber-framed walls) have become more common.

8.3.3 Hollow Clay Block Walls

Hollow clay blocks perform well thermally and range in thickness from 140–365 mm (5½–14⅜"). This performance is helped by a thin mortar-jointing system. Some blocks come with insulation inserted into the voids, increasing their ability to retain heat. However, they have less strength than standard block and cannot be used below DPC level.

Fig. 167

1. External render
2. Hollow clay block
3. Airtightness layer
4. Service cavity
5. Internal wall finish

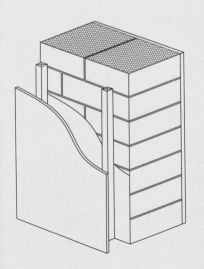

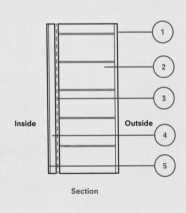

Inside   Outside

Section

8.3.4 Insulated Concrete Formwork

Insulated concrete formwork (ICF) is a system of formwork for reinforced concrete, usually made with a rigid thermal insulation that stays in place as a permanent interior and exterior feature for walls.

The insulation forms an interlocking series of modular units fitted together and filled with concrete. The units lock together and create a form for the structural walls of a building.

Fig. 168

1. Insulation/formwork
2. Poured concrete
3. Wall tie
4. External render
5. Service cavity
6. Internal finish

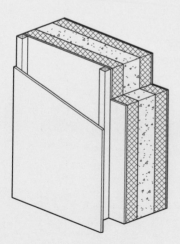

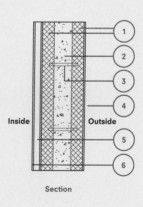

Inside   Outside

Section

8.3.5 Concrete Sandwich-panel Wall

Sandwich-panel construction involves two layers of concrete with an intermediate layer of rigid insulation. The outer and inner concrete walls are tied together at regular intervals across the insulation-filled cavity.

Sandwich-panel walls tend to be precast off site and are used where multiple walls are required for large builds. They are fixed together on site.

It is possible to form a sandwich-panel wall on site. However, it is a time-consuming and technically difficult process, which makes it expensive.

Fig. 169

1. Inner-leaf concrete

2. Insulation

3. Outer-leaf concrete

4. Wall tie

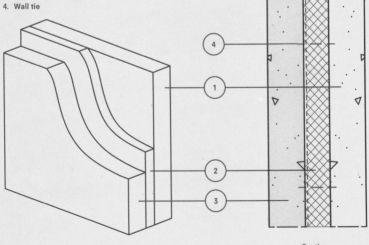

Section

8.3.6 Earth Walls

Building with earth is a technique that has been in use globally for thousands of years.

The ingredients added to the earth and the methods of construction vary from place to place, and depend very much on available soil type, local climate, and traditional skills and technologies employed. Other materials are often added to the earth to help bind it together.

This construction method has seen a decline in many parts of the world over the last 100 years because it is labour intensive, but there are signs of a resurgence due to its sustainable properties and attractive appearance. It is sometimes used in combination with timber-frame elements for added structural integrity.

Fig. 170

Earth wall construction

8.3.7 Timber (Wood) Frame with Masonry Cladding

Masonry (brick, rendered blockwork, composite panels or stone) can be used as an outer layer to protect a timber-framed building against weathering.

A ventilated cavity of air is needed to allow any moisture or water that finds its way into the cavity to drain out.

The breather membrane protects the insulation and timbers by allowing moisture that gets into the wall (most likely from outside) to escape. The location of the breather membrane will vary depending on local climate.

The airtight membrane prevents moisture in the internal air of the building from passing into the wall.

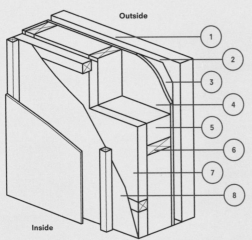

Outside

Inside

Fig. 171

1. Masonry wall cladding
2. Ventilated cavity
3. Breather membrane
4. Sheathing board
5. Insulation
6. Timber stud
7. Airtight membrane
8. Internal lining

Sheathing board is integral to the
stability of the timber-framed wall,
as it provides strength and stiffness.
Common sheathing materials
include OSB and plywood.

In order to avoid cold bridging
where the vertical studs occur,
an additional layer of insulation
can be fixed to the inside face
of the stud wall.

Fig. 172

1. Masonry wall cladding
2. Ventilated cavity
3. Breather membrane
4. Sheathing board
5. Insulation
6. Primary load-bearing wall
7. Airtight membrane
8. Internal lining
9. Service cavity

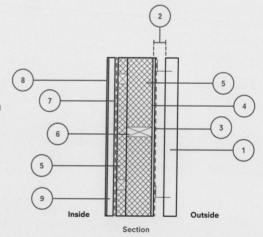

Inside   Outside

Section

8.3.8 Timber Frame with Supported Cladding

When cladding with timber externally, it is necessary to consider the direction of the cladding timbers because a ventilated cavity must be maintained to avoid build-up of moisture.

With horizontal cladding, the battens run vertically behind (see Fig. 173), while vertical cladding requires additional counter-battens to achieve a continuous air cavity.

Counter-battens form a double layer of battens running both horizontally and vertically, which maintain a clear air gap.

Fig. 173

1. Horizontal timber cladding
2. Ventilated cavity and battens
3. Breather membrane
4. Sheathing board
5. Insulation
6. Timber stud
7. Vapour control layer
8. Internal lining

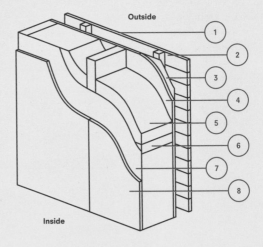

Outside

Inside

8.3.9 Structural Insulated Panels (SIPs)

SIPs are structural insulated panels that form a sandwich of rigid insulation with structural board cement adhered either side. The board can be sheet metal, plywood, cement or OSB, and the core is usually expanded polystyrene foam (EPS) or extruded polystyrene foam (XPS).

They are assembled offsite – saving on construction time – and can be used not only for walls but also for roofs and floors.

In the example shown here a brick wall is attached to the outside of the panel system with wall ties, forming the external finish.

Fig. 174

1. Airtight layer and service cavity
2. Cavity with breather membrane
3. Outer brick leaf
4. SIP

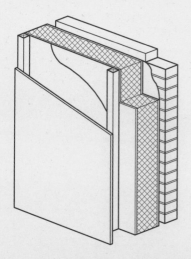

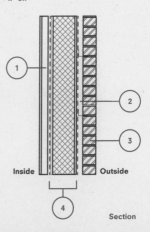

509

8.4
Roofs

Alongside the potential of roofs in terms of architectural expression, they form a critical component of the building envelope.

Roofs perform some basic functions. They must:

- keep out the rain
- help maintain the internal temperature of the building
- prevent both excessive heat loss and heat gain
- help stabilize the external walls
- provide sound protection to the interior of the building
- resist the spread of fire
- be strong enough to withstand the anticipated loads.

8.4.1 Flat (Low-Sloped) & Pitched Roofs

Roofs are divided into two clear categories: flat and pitched.

There are few totally flat roofs; most are slightly pitched to allow rainwater to run off. Flat roofs are classified as those with a pitch of 10° or less.

70° ≥ Wall

10°–70° = Pitched Roof

Flat Roof ≤ 10°

Pitched roofs are those between 10° and 70°. Any element sloped at more than 70° is classified as a wall.

Pitched roofs are sub-divided into shallow, medium and steep pitches. Any roof over 45° is considered steep, those between 30° and 45° are considered medium pitch, while those between 10° and 30° are a shallow pitch.

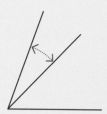

45°–70° = **Steep Pitch**

30°–45° = **Medium Pitch**

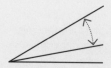

10°–30° = **Shallow Pitch**

8.4.2 Pitched Roofs

Mono-pitched Roof
The simplest form of pitched roof is one that slopes in one direction – a 'mono pitch'. The roof is supported by the walls below, and rain runs off it to the lower edge. Sometimes referred to as a shed roof.

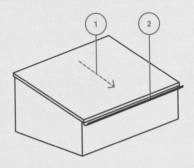

Fig. 175
1. Direction of flow of water
2. Rainwater collected in a gutter

Lean-to Roof
A mono-pitched roof that leans against a wall or structure is called a 'lean-to' roof. This is typically used for building types that are attached to main structures, such as sheds, greenhouses or small extensions. The structure of the roof runs from the larger structural wall to the lower wall of the lean-to element.

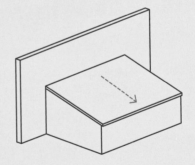

Simple Pitched Roof

This is the most common roof form. Two sloping planes meet at the ridge – the high point of the roof. Rain drains to the edges of the sloping planes. Sometimes referred to as a gable roof.

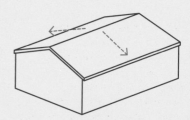

Butterfly Roof

In a butterfly roof, the sloped planes slope inwards and rain drains to a central gutter.

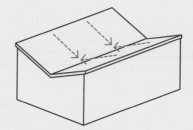

NB

The profile of the roof is determined by the following factors:

- Ease of construction: simple forms are easier to build.
- Span: mono-pitch and lean-to roofs are generally suitable for shorter spans than pitched or butterfly roofs.
- Aesthetic considerations.

8.4.3 Trusses

Today, pitched roofs are most commonly constructed with trusses. These are a series of parallel elements, assembled off site. The most common material for construction of trusses is timber, although steel is sometimes used to span greater distances.

There are a number of common timber truss shapes. 'Cut' roofs are made on site, whereas prefabricated roofs are made more economically off site but have certain limitations. Prefabricated roof trusses are more commonly used today.

Further information on trusses is given in **Section 7.2.10**.

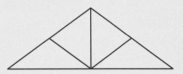

King post truss

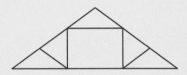

Queen post/Attic truss

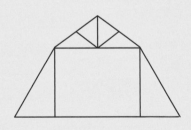

Mansard truss

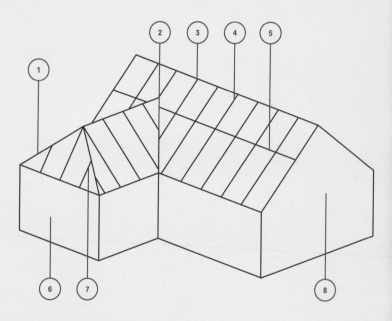

Fig. 176

1. Hip rafter
2. Valley rafter
3. Ridge
4. Common rafters (or trusses)
5. Purlin
6. Hipped gable
7. Jack rafter
8. Gable

8.4.4 Cut-roof Construction

Before the prefabrication of roof trusses, roofs were cut and assembled on site and are referred to as 'cut' roofs. In a typical pitched-roof construction, a series of parallel trusses sit on a timber wall plate, which rests on the external walls.

Fig. 177

1. Wall plate
2. Timber truss
3. Load-bearing wall

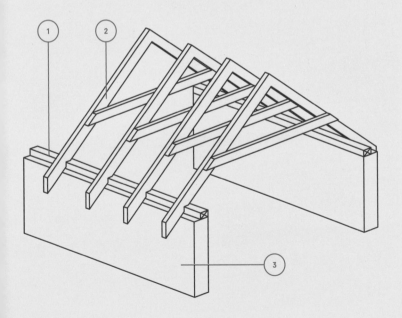

Trusses are braced to make them stable and minimize the impact of lateral loads.

Fig. 178

1. Horizontal bracing
2. Diagonal bracing
3. Ridge bracing

Three types of bracing are commonly used:

- ridge bracing
- diagonal bracing
- horizontal bracing –
  at the base of the truss or
  at the horizontal tie level.

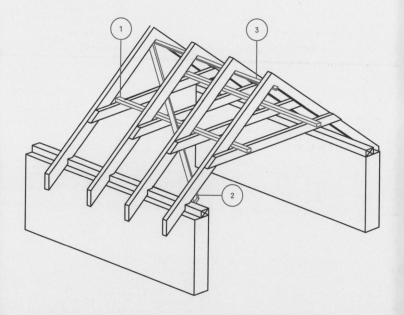

Insulation is fixed between the trusses and is covered with a waterproof membrane. This is fixed to the trusses.

The junction of the wall and roof is called the eaves junction (see **Section 8.5.5** for more detail).

A horizontal element fixed to the underside of the trusses' outer edge is called the soffit. This was traditionally made of timber, but other materials are sometimes used.

The fascia is the horizontal element fixed to the outer edge of the trusses. The gutter is often fixed to the fascia.

Small timber battens are then fixed across the trusses – through the waterproof layer. Tiles or slates are fixed to or hung from the battens.

Fig. 179

1. Waterproof membrane
2. Timber battens
3. Slates/tiles
4. Insulation
5. Gutter
6. Fascia
7. Soffit
8. Wall plate

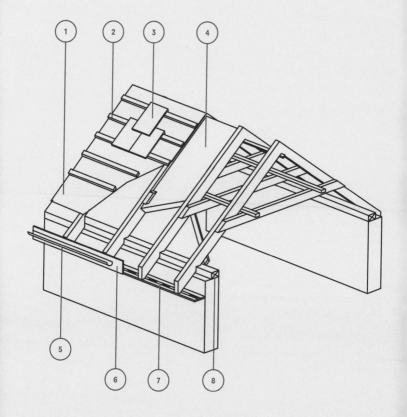

8.4.5 Roof Finishes

Typical roof finishes for pitched roofs in the UK and Ireland include:

- slate
- concrete tile
- clay tile
- sheet metal.

Other, less common roofing materials include:

- thatch
- timber shingles.

'Unit' roofing materials – i.e. those composed of small modular elements such as tiles and slates – are unsuitable for use on flat or shallow-pitched roofs. For more information on appropriate roof finishes, see **Chapter 6: Environment & Materials**.

Typical roof finishes for flat roofs include:

- bitumen and roofing felt
- asphalt
- single-ply membranes
- sheet metal
- thermoplastic sheeting
- sedum roofs
- grass.

8.4.6 Flat-roof Construction

Similar to internal upper-floor levels, roof construction can be slab construction (precast or cast in-situ), timber joists or composite metal decking. In domestic construction, timber-joist flat-roof construction is the most common.

Almost all flat roofs accommodate some slope to allow rainwater run-off. The recommended slope is 1 in 40 (known as the 'fall' of the roof). It is good practice to allow rainwater to run off in the shorter dimension of a flat roof.

For example, in a roof measuring 6 × 3m (20 × 10') the optimal solution would be to design so that the slope is across the 3m (10') dimension.

A wall upstand at the edge of a roof is called a parapet. A parapet is commonly topped by a coping, which can be of metal, stone or concrete.

The verge is the edge of the roof running with the fall, while the fascia runs perpendicular to the fall. The gutter is usually fixed to the fascia.

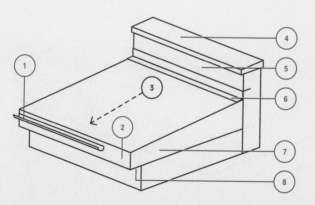

Fig. 180

1. Gutter
2. Fascia
3. Fall
4. Coping
5. Parapet
6. Flashing
7. Verge
8. Soffit

8.4.7 Flat-roof Build-ups

Cold-deck Roof

In this flat-roof system, the insulation is positioned between the joists with the decking and waterproof layer above. Because the decking is above the insulation, it is 'cold', hence the term 'cold-deck roof'.

A critical factor in the success of the cold-deck roof is that there must be a minimum of 50 mm (2") clear ventilation space above the insulation, ventilated on both sides. This is to prevent a build-up of moisture, which could cause the timbers to rot and the insulation to become saturated.

The advantage of positioning the insulation between the joists is that the overall thickness of the slab is reduced, making a thin roof profile.

Fig. 181

1. Waterproof membrane
2. Joists
3. Roof decking (typically marine plywood or OSB)
4. Ventilated cavity
5. Plasterboard
6. Insulation
7. Vapour barrier/ airtight layer

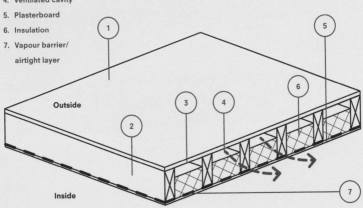

Warm-deck Roof

In this flat-roof system, the insulation is positioned above the joists and decking with the waterproof layer above. Because the decking is below the insulation, it is 'warm'.

Ventilation is not necessary in the warm-deck roof as the air between the joists is the same temperature as the internal room temperature and not prone to condensation. The build-up of a warm-deck roof is thicker than that of a cold deck roof. Warm-deck roofs require continuous support from the decking layer. Roof falls are achieved by tapering the insulation or inserting firring pieces (tapered lengths of timber batten, also known as furring in the US).

Fig. 182

1. Waterproof membrane
2. Roof decking (typically marine plywood or OSB)
3. Joists
4. Insulation
5. Vapour control layer
6. Plasterboard and airtight layer

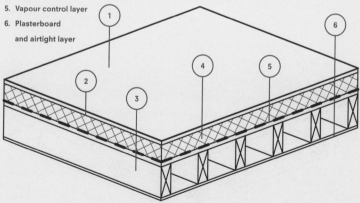

Concrete Warm-deck Roof

This type of flat roof can be constructed with a cast in-situ or precast slab. Insulation sits above the slab.

In order to achieve a fall, a screed can be laid to falls on top of the insulation.

Concrete slabs can be used for larger spans than timber-joist flat roofs, but are more expensive to construct.

Fig. 183

1. Waterproof membrane
2. Insulation
3. Concrete slab
4. Screed laid to falls

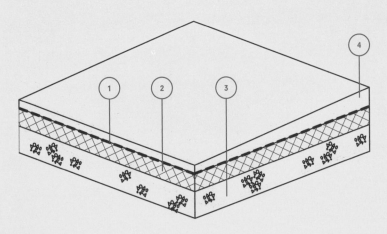

Inverted Warm-deck Roof

In this flat-roof system, the insulation is positioned above the the joists, decking and waterproof layer. It is a variant on the standard warm-deck roof (see p. 525).

Because the insulation is above the waterproof layer, it is allowed to get wet. Therefore specialist insulation must be used, as the performance of most forms of insulation is dramatically reduced by water saturation.

The insulation must also be weighed down with ballast to prevent it becoming dislodged during storms. This ballast can be in the form of concrete paving slabs or gravel.

Fig. 184

1. Roof decking (typically marine plywood or OSB)
2. Joists
3. Waterproof membrane
4. Ballast
5. Insulation
6. Plasterboard and airtight layer

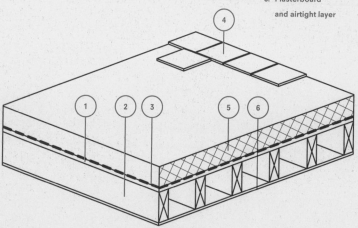

8.5
Openings
& Junctions

Critical to the success of a building envelope are openings and junctions. The junctions between elements such as walls and floors should be detailed to prevent these becoming weak points in the thermal and environmental enclosure. Openings such as windows and doors must be designed to allow movement of light, air and people, without giving rise to problems of thermal breaks or water ingress. In the following pages we include some key junction details. Bear in mind that the technical details will vary according to the building materials you use, the insulation requirements and the nature of the construction system.

8.5.1 Forming an Opening

In order to form an opening in a wall, whether it is a door or a window, it is necessary to insert a structural element that spans the opening. This element, usually a lintel, carries the load of the wall above the opening and spreads it to the walls on either side. A lintel can be made of timber, steel or concrete depending on the type of wall it is in and the loads it needs to carry.

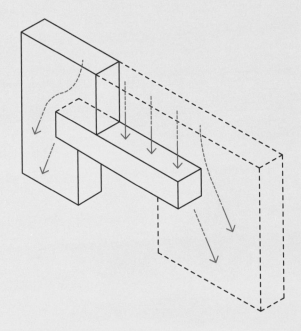

8.5.2 Lintel in Timber-(Wood-) framed Wall

In timber-frame construction, the method of forming an opening in a wall is different. A number of additional timber elements are inserted into the stud wall to make the opening.

Trimmer studs strengthen the stud vertically. Cripple studs provide additional vertical support.

What is known as a double header (two timbers spanning the opening) is positioned above the opening to form a window head or lintel.

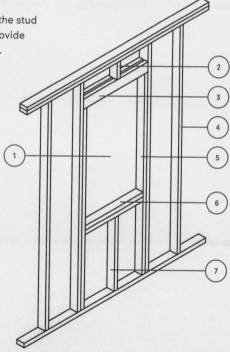

Fig. 185

1. Opening
2. Short cripple
3. Double header
4. Typical stud
5. Trimmer stud
6. Sill (cill)
7. Cripple stud

8.5.3 Window-head Junction (in a Full-fill Cavity Wall)

An insulated pressed-metal lintel will carry both the inner and outer leaves across a window or door opening. The benefit of these lintels is that they are pre-insulated and come in standard sizes.

The line of thermal insulation must join up with the window frame (as it does in this detail) to avoid creating a cold bridge.

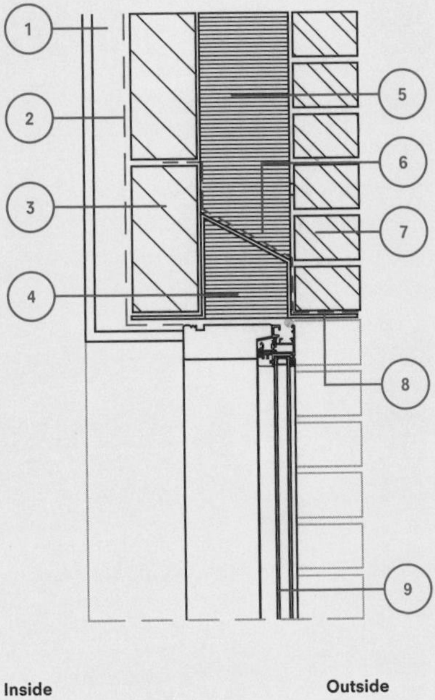

Fig. 186

1. Service cavity
2. Airtight layer
3. Inner block wall
4. Insulated lintel
5. Insulation
6. Stepped DPC
7. Brick outer leaf
8. Weep holes
9. Window

Inside

Outside

8.5.4 Window-cill (Sill) Junction (in a Full-fill Cavity Wall)

When we take a large-scale section through the window at window cill level, we call it a 'cill detail' (also sometimes spelled 'sill'). Again, the critical issues here are continuity of the thermal layer and the avoidance of water penetration.

The window and the cill must be designed to carry water away from the wall to prevent water ingress. This detail shows a cavity wall with a pressed-metal cill and timber-and-metal window.

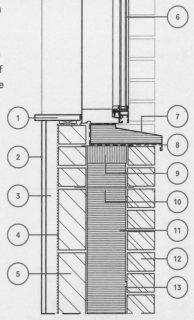

Fig. 187

1. Internal window cill (sill)
2. Internal finish
3. Service cavity
4. Airtight layer
5. Inner block wall
6. Window
7. External insulated cill (sill)
8. DPC
9. Cavity closer
10. Wall tie
11. Insulation
12. Brick outer leaf
13. 10mm/⅜" cavity

Inside

Outside

8.5.5 Pitched-roof Eaves Junction

Fig. 188

1. Airtight layer
2. Cavity closer
3. Inner block wall
4. Insulation
5. Insulated lintel
6. Window
7. Air flow
8. Stepped DPC
9. Brick outer leaf

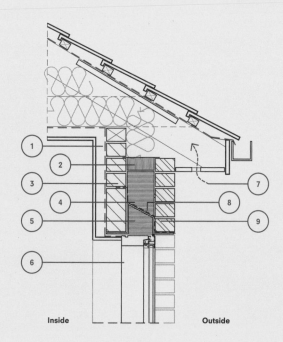

Inside   Outside

Where an external wall meets a roof, this junction is known as either an eaves or a parapet junction depending on whether the edge of the roof projects beyond the line of the wall or sits behind an upstand in the wall.

In the roof build-up, a continuous airflow is critical to the performance of the roof. The flow of air ensures the movement of moisture out of the structure, avoiding condensation.

8.5.6 Flat-roof Parapet Junction

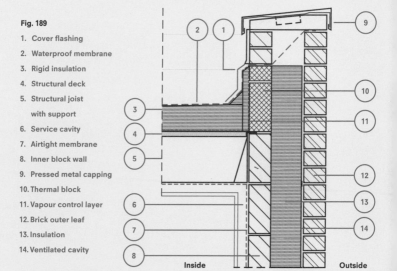

Fig. 189

1. Cover flashing
2. Waterproof membrane
3. Rigid insulation
4. Structural deck
5. Structural joist
   with support
6. Service cavity
7. Airtight membrane
8. Inner block wall
9. Pressed metal capping
10. Thermal block
11. Vapour control layer
12. Brick outer leaf
13. Insulation
14. Ventilated cavity

Inside   Outside

With a flat roof, a continuous airflow is not required when constructing a warm-deck flat roof.

A waterproof membrane is applied in this instance to the flat-roof area with a minimum 150mm upstand, again to protect against a build-up of water entering the building.

A sloped 'capping' to the top of the wall also helps to direct water onto the roof and away from the building façade.

8.5.7 Door Threshold Junction

The junction between inside and outside at floor level is known as the threshold.

A level threshold occurs when the ground level outside and the finished floor level inside are the same.

This continuity in level is important for the building in use, as it allows all users to access the building by avoiding the need for steps.

In the detail shown in Fig. 190, the damp-proof membrane (DPM/radon barrier) above the slab is lapped with the damp-proof course (DPC). This prevents water from entering the building. A drain directly outside the door frame gathers any water from the surrounding ground and the door glazing.

Fig. 190

1. Screed
2. Insulation
3. Slab
4. DPM/radon barrier
5. Internal floor finish
6. Drain
7. Sand blinding
8. External finish
9. Lapped DPM and DPC
10. Hardcore
11. Rigid insulation EPS 300

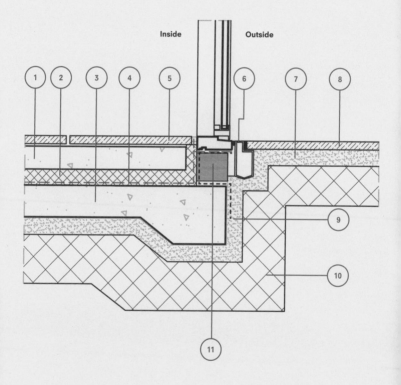

Inside   Outside

① ② ③ ④ ⑤ ⑥ ⑦ ⑧

⑨

⑩

⑪

References &
Further Reading

References for Chapter Opener Quotes

Chapter 1: Getting Started in Architecture

Heidegger, Martin (1977) *Basic Writings*. New York: Harper & Row, p. 357.

Pallasmaa, Juhani (2009) *The Thinking Hand: Existential and embodied wisdom in architecture*. Chichester, West Sussex: John Wiley & Sons, p. 52.

Chapter 2: Principles of Representation

Evans, Robin (1986) *Translations from Drawing to Building* (AA Files, No 12, Summer). London: Architectural Association, p. 3.

Chapter 3: Drawing Techniques

Frascari, Marco (2007) 'Introduction'. In: Marco Frascari, Jonathan Hale and Bradley Starkey (eds), *From Models to Drawings*. London: Routledge, p. 3.

Chapter 4: Working Through Drawing

Brown, Christopher (2008) 'Straight Lines'. In: Marc Treib (ed.), *Drawing/Thinking: Confronting an electronic age*. London and New York: Routledge, p. 142.

Chapter 5: Surveying

Bannister, Arthur, Raymond, Stanley and Baker, Raymond (1998) *Surveying*. Harlow: Longman Ltd, p. 1.

Chapter 6: Environment & Materials

Manfred Sack, quoted by Deplazes, Andrea (2008) *Constructing Architecture: Materials, processes, structures – a handbook*. Basel: Birkhauser, p. 19.

Chapter 7: Structure

Balmond, Cecil (2002) *Informal*. Munich: Prestel, p. 13.

Chapter 8: Principles of Construction

Auguste Perret, quoted by Frampton, Kenneth (1995) *Studies in Tectonic Culture: The poetics of construction in nineteenth and twentieth century architecture*. Joint publication of Graham Foundation for Advanced Studies in the Fine Arts and The MIT Press, p. 153.

Further Reading

Chapter 1: Getting Started in Architecture

Bielefeld, Bert and Skiba, Isabella (2007) *Basics Series: Technical Drawing*. Basel: Birkhauser.

Reekie, Fraser (1976) *Draftsmanship* (3rd edition). London: Edward Arnold. [Ch 1]

Schilling, Alexander (2007) *Basics Series: Model building*. Basel: Birkhauser.

Chapter 2: Principles of Representation

Reekie, Fraser (1976) *Draftsmanship* (3rd edition). London: Edward Arnold. [Chs 3 & 8]

Zell, Mo (2008) *The Architectural Drawing Course: Understand the principles and master the practices.* London: Thames & Hudson. [Chs 3, 4 & 9]

Chapter 3: Drawing Techniques

Adler, David (1999) *Metric Handbook: Planning and Design Data*. Oxford: Architectural Press.

Baden-Powell, Charlotte (2001) *Architect's Pocket Book*. Oxford: Architectural Press. [See pp. 29–32]

Bielefeld, Bert and Skiba, Isabella (2007) *Basics Series: Technical Drawing*. Basel: Birkhauser.

Department of the Environment, Heritage and Local Government. *Technical Guidance Documents. Document K: Stairways, ladders, ramps and guards*. Available at: www.environ.ie/en/TGD

Hall, Dennis and Giglio, Nina (2016) *Architectural Graphic Standards* (12th edition). Hoboken, NJ: John Wiley.

Hochberg, Annette, Hafke, Jan-Henrik and Raab, Joachim (2009) *Scale Open Close: Windows, doors, gates, loggias, filters*. Basel: Birkhauser.

Reekie, Fraser (1976) *Draftsmanship* (3rd edition). London: Edward Arnold.[Chs 4 & 6]

Chapter 4: Working Through Drawing

Cook, P. (2014) *Drawing: the Motive Force of Architecture*. Chichester, West Sussex: John Wiley & Sons.

Cullen, Gordon (1961) *The Concise Townscape*. London: Routledge.

Farrelly, L. (2008). *Basics Architecture 01: Representational Techniques* (Vol. 1). Lausanne, Switzerland: AVA Publishing.

Lewis, P., Tsurumaki, M., and Lewis, D. J. (2016) *Manual of Section*. Hudson, New York: Princeton Architectural Press.

Reekie, Fraser (1976) *Draftsmanship* (3rd edition). London: Edward Arnold. [Chs 9 & 10]

Zell, Mo (2008) *The Architectural Drawing Course: Understand the principles and master the practices.* London: Thames & Hudson. [Chs 1, 2 & 6]

Chapter 5: Surveying

Bannister, Arthur, Raymond, Stanley, and Baker, Raymond (1998) *Surveying*. Harlow: Longman Ltd.

Heywood, Huw (2013) *101 Rules of Thumb for Low Energy Architecture*. London: RIBA Publishing.

Pelsmakers, Sophie (2015) *Environmental Design Pocketbook*. London: RIBA Publishing.

Whyte, W.S. (1997) *Basic Surveying* (4th edition). London: Butterworth-Heinemann.

Chapter 6: Environment & Materials

Baden-Powell, Charlotte (2001) *Architect's Pocket Book*. Oxford: Architectural Press.

Dean, Yvonne (1996) *Materials Technology,* Mitchell's Building Series. Harlow: Longman Ltd.

Deplazes, Andrea (2008) *Constructing Architecture: Materials, Processes, Structures –*
   A Handbook. Basel: Birkhauser.

Heywood, Huw (2013) *101 Rules of Thumb For Low Energy Architecture*. London: RIBA Publishing.

Koralturk, A. Togay (2016) *LEED Green Associate Complete Study Guide*. LDCT Publications.

Pelsmakers, Sofie (2015) *The Environmental Design Pocketbook*. London: RIBA Publishing.

Specific Materials References (as mentioned in text)

Bennet, David (2006–2008) *Concrete Elegance*, Volumes 1–4. London: RIBA Publishing.

Campbell, James W. P. (2003) *Brick: A World History*. London: Thames & Hudson.

Curran, Joanne (2010) *Stone by Stone – A Guide to Building Stone in the Northern Ireland Environment*.
   Belfast: Appletree Press.

Dean, Yvonne (1996) *Mitchell's Building Series: Materials technology*. Harlow: Longman Ltd.
   [See Chapter 13]

Deplazes, Andrea (2008) *Constructing Architecture: Materials, Processes, Structures –*
   A Handbook. Basel: Birkhauser. [See pp. 77–112]

Fröhlich, Burkhard and Schulenburg, Sonja (2003) *Metal Architecture: Design and Construction*.
   Basel: Birkhauser.

Hugues, Theodor, Steiger, Ludwig and Weber, Johann (2005) *Dressed Stone: Types of Stone, Details,*
   Examples. Basel: Birkhauser

Kaltenbach, Frank (2004) *Translucent Materials: Glass, Plastics, Metals*. Basel: Birkhauser.

Krewinkel, Heinz W. (1998) *Glass Buildings: Material, Structure and Detail*. Basel: Birkhauser.

Pfeifer, Günter, Liebers, Antje M. and Brauneck, Per (2005) *Exposed Concrete: Technology and Design*.
   Basel: Birkhauser.

Pfeifer, Günter, Ramke, Rolf, Achtziger, Joachim and Zilch, Konrad (2001) *Masonry Construction Manual*.
   Basel: Birkhauser.

Pfundstein, Margit (2008) *Insulating Materials: Principles, Materials, Applications*.
    Basel: Birkhauser.

Reichel, Alexander, Hochberg, Annette and Koepke, Christine (2004) *Plaster, Render, Paint and
    Coatings: Details, Products, Case studies*. Basel: Birkhauser.

Wood Marketing Federation of Ireland (2001) *Woodspec: A guide to designing, detailing and
    specifying timber in Ireland*. Wicklow: Wood Marketing Federation of Ireland.

Chapter 7: Structure

Ching, Francis D. K., Onoyue, Barry and Zuberbuhler, Douglas (2009) *Building Structures Illustrated:
    Patterns, systems and design*. Hoboken, NJ: John Wiley.

Cobb, Fiona (2009) *Structural Engineer's Pocket Book*. Oxford:
    Butterworth-Heinemann.

Cruvellier, Mark R., Eggen, Arne P. and Sandaker, Bjorn N. (2019) *The Structural Basis of Architecture*
    (3rd edition). London: Taylor & Francis Ltd.

Deplazes, Andrea (2008) *Constructing Architecture: Materials, Processes, Structures – A Handbook*.
    Basel: Birkhauser.

Hunt, Tony (2003) *Tony Hunt's Structures Notebook* (2nd edition). Oxford: Architectural Press.

Moussavi, Farshid (2010) *The Function of Form*. New York: Actar.

Silver, Pete and McLean, Will (2021) Introduction to Architectural Technology (3rd edition). London:
    Laurence King Publishing.

Stacey, Michael (2010) *Concrete: A studio design guide*. London: RIBA Publishing.

Chapter 8: Principles of Construction

Allen, Edward and Iano, Joseph (2017) *The Architect's Studio Companion: Rules of Thumb for
    Preliminary Design* (6th edition). Hoboken, NJ: John Wiley.

Ching, Francis D. K. (2011) *A Visual Dictionary of Architecture*. Hoboken, NJ: John Wiley.

Ching, Francis D. K. (2008) *Building Construction Illustrated* (4th edition). Hoboken, NJ: John Wiley.

Ching, Francis D. K. (2009) *Building Structures Illustrated: Patterns, systems, and design*. Hoboken, NJ:
    John Wiley.

Deplazes, Andrea (2008) *Constructing Architecture: Materials, Processes, Structures – A Handbook*.
    Basel: Birkhauser.

Ford, Edward R. (1996) *The Details of Modern Architecture*. Cambridge, MA: MIT Press.

Foster, J.S. and Greeno, Roger (2007) *Mitchell's Building Series. Part 2:
    Structure & Fabric* (7th edition). Harlow: Pearson Prentice Hall.

Index

Acknowledgements & Credits

We would like to acknowledge the following people who have enabled this book to happen. Sincere thanks to: **Hugh Campbell** and **John Tuomey** for their input and support; **Sarah Lappin**, our advising editor, who has made insightful and clear comments all of which have helped strengthen the book; **Gerry Cahill, Wendy Barrett** and all the staff and students in UCD School of Architecture who have contributed to the book.

Conor & David, the graphic design studio, for their love of craft and their professionalism.

Finally thanks to **Dermot Boyd** for his advice and **Catherine Gorman** and **Peter Dawson** for their positive words.

On the publication of the second edition, we wish to thank our editor at Laurence King, **Liz Faber**, for her rigorous attention and positive support throughout. Thank you too to **David Fannon** for his advice and assistance on making this book accessible and useful to American students. Finally, thank you to **Detail** graphic designers for their work in updating and revising the content and layout.

Images are listed by page number.
Any images not listed were supplied by the authors and designers of the book.

T = Top
B = Bottom
C = Centre
L = Left
R = Right

61, 62, 63 Courtesy University College Dublin (UCD)

64L UCD/3D Printer

64R, 65, 66L UCD

66R Edwin Jebb/UCD

67 UCD

70R Courtesy Bolton Adhesives

75L Image of FIMO® Soft Block, Provided by Staedtler (UK) Ltd.

93 Henk Snoek, Courtesy of Simon Walker

216–17 Sketch courtesy of Dermot Boyd

218–19 Sketch courtesy of Michael Pike

220–21 Sketch courtesy of Gerry Cahill

229 Killian Doherty, Architectural Field Office

230, 231 Caryn Chan/UCD

236 Conor Maguire

237 Conor McGowan, Piero Giovannini, Federica Zoboli, Francesca Liebowitz, Liliana Tubak, Beatrice Gambato, Nelly Vitello, Ilaria Saggese, Carolina Biascia

238 Gorman Architects/Sean Lynch

239 Emer O'Daly, O'Daly Architects

242–55 Courtesy of FKL Architects

254 Verena Henze, courtesy of FKL Architects

258 Paper sketch model of University Campus UTEC Lima, Peru, Grafton Architects

259 Contour site model, Boyd Cody Architects

260 Site model, Architecture Students, TUDublin

262 Display Model, Barcelona Pavilion by Mies van der Rohe/UCD

265 Large-scale façade and interior study model, Courtesy Boyd Cody Architects

266 Presentation model, Courtesy Boyd Cody Architects

302 © Ordnance Survey Ireland/Government of Ireland, Copyright Permit No. MP 000315

327 Gemma Gallagher/UCD

432 shutterstock.com/Parnumas Na Phatthalung

433 shutterstock.com

450 Ros Kavanagh, Courtesy Grafton Architects

451–53 Courtesy Grafton Architects

460 Ros Kavanagh, Courtesy Grafton Architects

461 © Dennis Gilbert/VIEW, Courtesy Grafton Architects

475 Courtesy of Cormac Allen

489 & 491 Drawn by Harry Bancroft. Illustrations based on originals from Kore + Viking

502–503 Drawn by Harry Bancroft

506–509 Drawn by Harry Bancroft

Anne Gorman, MRIAI, MSc, BArch
Anne has been studying, practising and teaching architecture and technology for over 30 years. She began her career draughting before she graduated from the Dublin Institute of Technology (Dip. Construction) in 1993, University College Dublin (BArch) in 2002 and from UCL (MSc. Light and Lighting) in 2015. Anne has taught architecture and architectural technology at University College Dublin and the Dublin School of Architecture, Technological University Dublin.

Miriam Delaney, MRIAI, MA, BArch
Miriam is an architect and lecturer, with 15 years of experience teaching architecture. She graduated from University College Dublin (BArch) in 2003 and from UCL (MA Arch. History) in 2011. Miriam has taught architecture in UCD, Queens University Belfast, and currently teaches at the Dublin School of Architecture, Technological University Dublin. She represented Ireland as part of the 'Free Market' team at the 2018 Venice Architecture Biennale.

Advising Editor for first edition:
Dr. Sarah A. Lappin is Head of Architecture at Queen's University Belfast.

US Advisor for second edition:
David Fannon, Associate Professor, School of Architecture and Department of Civil and Environmental Engineering, Northeastern University, Boston.